Genre and the Language Learning Classroom

Brian Paltridge

Ann Arbor

THE UNIVERSITY OF MICHIGAN PRESS

Copyright © by the University of Michigan 2001
All rights reserved
Published in the United States of America by
The University of Michigan Press
Manufactured in the United States of America
♾ Printed on acid-free paper

2004   2003   2002   2001   4   3   2   1

A CIP catalog record for this book is available from the British Library.

Library of Congress Cataloging-in-Publication Data

Paltridge, Brian, 1947–
    Genre and the language learning classroom / Brian Paltridge.
       p.   cm.
    Includes bibliographical references and index.
    ISBN 0-472-08804-1 (pbk. : alk. paper)
    1. English language—Study and teaching—Foreign speakers. 2. Language and languages—Study and teaching. 3. Literary form—Study and teaching. I. Title.
PE1128.A2 P285   2001
428′.0071—dc21

                                                              2001002843

Acknowledgments

Many people have influenced my thinking and writing about genre. In particular, I thank Winifred Crombie, Suzanne Eggins, Jim Martin, and David Butt for what I have learned from them and for the various ways in which they have supported what I have done. Others were extremely helpful at crucial stages in the development of this book. Among these, I especially thank Ann Johns, Vijay Bhatia, and Jack Richards. Closer to home, I am grateful to Frances Christie, Tim McNamara, Kieran O'Loughlin, and Alastair Pennycook for their interest in and support for my work. At the University of Michigan Press, I am especially grateful to Kelly Sippell for her clear and helpful advice, as well as to the anonymous reviewers of my manuscript for their detailed and helpful comments.

In addition, I thank the following organizations for allowing their works to be included in the text.

Cambridge University Press for the excerpt reprinted with permission from *Writing for Study Purposes: A Teacher's Guide to Developing Individual Writing Skills,* by A. Brookes and P. Grundy, © 1990 by Cambridge University Press; for the excerpts reprinted with permission from *Active Listening: Expanding Understanding through Content, Student's Book 3,* by M. Helgesen, S. Brown, and D. Smith, © 1996 by Cambridge University Press. Reprinted with the permission of Cambridge University Press.

Oxford University Press for the excerpt reprinted with permission from *Discourse,* by Guy Cook, © 1989 by Oxford University Press. Reprinted by permission of Oxford University Press.

National Centre for English Language Teaching and Research (NCELTR), Macquarie University, Australia, for the diagram reproduced with permission from *English for Social Purposes: A Handbook for Teachers of Adult Literacy,* by J. Hammond, A. Burns, H. Joyce, D. Brosnan, and L. Gerot, based on a concept by M. Callaghan and J. Rothery, © 1992 by Macquarie University; for the worksheet reproduced with permission from "Keeping a Conversation Going," by B. Paltridge, *Prospect* 3 (1): 107–8, © 1987 by Macquarie University; for the table reproduced with permission from *Focus on Speaking,* by

A. Burns and H. Joyce, p. 79, © 1997 by Macquarie University; for the extracts adapted with permission from *I See What You Mean: Using Spoken Discourse in the Classroom,* by A. Burns, H. Joyce, and S. Gollin, © 1996 by Macquarie University. Reproduced with permission from the National Centre for English Language Teaching and Research (NCELTR), Australia.

TESOL for the excerpt reprinted with permission from "Reading across the Curriculum: A Genre-Based Perspective," by B. Paltridge, in D. Short, ed., *New Ways in Teaching English at the Secondary Level,* © 1999 by TESOL; for the excerpt reprinted with permission from "Observation, Feedback, and Setting Individual Learning Goals," by B. Paltridge, in J. D. Brown, ed., *New Ways of Classroom Assessment,* © 1998 by TESOL.

SEAMEO Regional Language Centre for the excerpt reprinted with permission from "A Genre Description of the Argumentative Essay," by Ken Hyland, *RELC Journal* 21 (1), © 1990 by SEAMEO Regional Language Centre.

Text Productions for the excerpts reprinted with permission from *Context— Text—Grammar: Teaching the Genres and Grammar of School Writing in Infants and Primary Classrooms,* by P. Knapp and M. Watkins, © 1994 by Text Productions.

New South Wales Adult Migrant Education Service Publications for the tables reproduced with permission from *Certificate in Spoken and Written English,* by P. Hagan, S. Hood, E. Jackson, M. Jones, H. Joyce, and M. Manidis, 2d ed., © 1993 by New South Wales Adult Migrant Education Service Publications; for the table reproduced with permission from *Workplace Texts in the Language Classroom,* by H. Joyce, © 1992 by New South Wales Adult Migrant Education Service Publications.

Elsevier Science for the tables reprinted with permission from "EAP Placement Testing: An Integrated Approach," by B. Paltridge, *English for Specific Purposes* 11 (3), © 1992 by Elsevier Science; for the extract reprinted with permission from "Analysing Genre: A Relational Perspective," by B. Paltridge, *System* 23 (4), © 1995 by Elsevier Science. Reprinted with permission from Elsevier Science.

AEE Publishers for the excerpt reprinted with permission from *Making Sense of Functional Grammar,* by L. Gerot and P. Wignell, © 1994 by L. Gerot and P. Wignell.

Every effort has been made to trace the ownership of all copyrighted material in this book and to obtain permission for its use.

Contents

Chapter 1

Introduction

Overview: Genre and the Language Learning Classroom

This chapter provides a brief overview of the main approaches to genre analysis within the context of language teaching and learning. The remainder of the book is devoted to discussing ways in which insights gained in each of these perspectives might be taken up in the language learning classroom. Chapter 2 considers ways in which genre might be considered as an organizing principle for language learning programs. It includes a discussion of a particular teaching and learning cycle that is often drawn on in systemic-oriented classrooms but that also might usefully be drawn on in classrooms working with other views of language. Chapter 3 suggests ways in which the relationship between genre and context might be taken up in the language learning classroom. Chapter 4 looks at discourse structures and suggests ways in which these might be focused on in the language learning classroom. Chapter 5 presents suggestions for focusing on genre-specific language in the language learning classroom. It includes a proposal for a genre-based view of grammar that draws from systemic genre work but that might equally be drawn on in other views of genre as well. Chapter 6 discusses the principles of genre-based assessment and provides suggestions for how genre-based assessment might be considered in language learning classrooms. The final chapter of the book considers directions for further research and development in the area of applied genre studies, as well as some of the possible limitations of genre-based instruction.

Each chapter in the book concludes with tasks and discussion questions that focus on the content of the chapter. These are followed by suggestions for further reading that will provide further depth to the aspects of genre analysis and instruction that have been introduced in the chapter.

Why Genre?

Recent years have seen increased attention given to the notion of genre in the area of language teaching and learning. This is especially the case in the teaching of English for specific purposes (ESP), in composition studies in North American colleges and universities, and in Australia in the areas of language learning in schools and adult settings involving first and second languages.

The term *genre* was first introduced in the area of ESP in 1981, in an *ESP Journal* article by Elaine Tarone and her colleagues on the language of scientific research reports and in Swales's (1981) study of introductions to scientific reports. The Australian work on genre dates back to a similar time and originates in the examination of children's writing in Australian elementary-school classrooms. Genre studies in composition studies and in what is often called the "new rhetoric" has been influenced, in particular, by an essay written by speech communications specialist Carolyn Miller in 1984 titled "Genre as Social Action" and has been discussed in relation to freshman writing and professional communication in North American settings.

In ESP genre work, the term *genre* refers to a class of communicative events, such as, for example, a seminar presentation, a university lecture, or an academic essay. In "systemic" genre work, a genre is more often referred to as a kind of text, such as a description, procedure, or exposition. In new rhetoric work, genres are often described as events or social actions that help people interpret and create particular texts. ESP and Australian genre studies have mostly examined the language, discourse, and, more recently, contextual features of genres, whereas new rhetoric genre studies have focused mostly on the social, cultural, and institutional contexts of particular genres, rather than on their formal features.

ESP genre studies are based largely on John Swales's (1981, 1990) work on the discourse structure and linguistic features of scientific reports. These studies have had a strong influence in the teaching of ESP and especially the teaching of academic writing to ESL graduate students. Australian genre work is based on the work of such linguists as Michael Halliday, Ruqaiya Hasan, and Jim Martin and on their "systemic functional" theory of language. This theory describes language in terms of the choices a speaker or writer makes from the language system in particular contexts of use. These choices are described in functional, rather than grammatical, terms—hence, the term *systemic functional*.

Genre studies aim to draw together language, content, and the context of discourse production and interpretation. They further aim to explain goal-oriented patterns of language use in terms of regularities of purpose, content, and form. Genre analysts also argue for the dynamic, rather than static, nature of genres. Thus, even though genres may, at times, seem conventional and relatively stable, they nonetheless evolve and change in response to changes in the context in which they occur as well as changes in communicative needs.

All instances of genres reflect certain ideologies or worldviews. These worldviews tend to be silent and hidden rather than explicitly stated. Genre is a somewhat abstract concept in that "you can see the text but not the genre" (Ongstad, personal communication with the author, March 1997). Thus, as Heather Kay (1995) observes, genres have a virtual existence. We draw strongly, however, on the concept of genre—in conjunction with the social and cultural context of a text— for both interpreting and creating particular meanings.

Different genres are also often closely related to each other. An example of this is the academic essay, which may draw from and cite many other genres, such as academic lectures, specialist academic texts, and journal articles. Academic essays are part of what Charles Bazerman (1994) calls a "system of genres," where one genre requires, or presupposes, the existence of another.

Genres provide ways for responding to recurring communicative situations. They further provide a frame that enables individuals to orient to and interpret particular communicative events. Making this genre knowledge explicit can provide language learners with the knowledge and skills they need to communicate successfully in particular discourse communities. It can also provide learners with access to socially powerful forms of language.

Genre and the Language Learning Program

Many arguments have been put forward in support of genre as an organizing principle for the development of language learning programs. As early as 1983, Henry Widdowson suggested that basing linguistic analysis on the notion of genre has a number of advantages over other frameworks for analysis. In particular, it takes us beyond the level of notions and functions into larger units of work on which to base our teaching and learning programs. A genre-based approach to language program development has the advantage that the units in a genre-based language learning program are neither too small, as in a structural or functional syllabus, nor too large, as in a skills-based syllabus. Units in a genre-based language learning program emphasize communicative purpose and allow for the demonstration of typical patterns of textual and linguistic organization (Swales 1986). A genre-based approach to language program development enables curriculum designers to group together texts that are similar in terms of purpose, organization, and audience. Further, it provides students with knowledge of the organizational and linguistic features of genres that they need to have command of in their academic disciplines and professions (Dudley-Evans 1989).

The notion of genre as being the "right size" for a unit on which to base language learning programs takes the principle of organization beyond grammatical or functional units yet excludes neither from the overall program. A genre-based approach to language program development starts with genre as the overall driving force of the syllabus yet still includes all other aspects of language—such as grammar, functions, vocabulary, and language skills—that one might expect to see in a communicative syllabus. This, combined with discussions of the role and purpose of genres and the context in which they occur, helps learners understand why genres are written or spoken the way they are (Johns 1997).

Systemic genre analysts argue that a genre-based perspective focuses on language at the level of whole text while at the same time taking into account the social and cultural context in which it is used. They argue, further, that the notion of genre as "a staged, goal-oriented purposeful activity" (Martin 1984, 25) relates language choices to cultural purpose by revealing the stages through which a user of a language moves to accomplish particular social and cultural goals. Thus, a genre-based approach to language program development moves from linguistic description to explanation and understanding of why genres are shaped the way they are and how they achieve their particular communicative goals (Bhatia 1993, 1995a).

Genre analysis should, however, remain descriptive and not prescriptive, as it sometimes has become. An overly prescriptive approach to language teaching based on the results of genre analysis can easily imply that students only have to learn basic textual structures to create a genre that meets the expectations of a particular discourse community (Dudley-Evans 1995a).

Nonetheless, genre analysis can provide students with both rhetorical and linguistic awareness of different genres, as well as a context in which both the general and particular expectations of different discourse communities can be explored. It is important, however, that teachers do not begin with analyses of decontextualized examples of genres but, rather, make it clear from the start that genres exist in and for particular discourse communities (Johns 1997). As Johns (1994) points out, teachers need to stress the purpose the genre serves and the context of production and interpretation of the text and to use this as the starting point for their discussion rather than commencing with isolated features of texts.

It is also important for teachers to recognize that they are teaching tendencies rather than fixed patterns of forms. Equally, teachers need to guard against leading students to the view that genres have tightly pre-scribed boundaries and that a text must be a member of either one genre category or another or, rather, an instance of what Vijay Bhatia (1997) terms *genre mixing* or *genre embedding*. The aim should not be to give students rigid templates against which all texts are then forced to fit (Swales 1990). Rather, it should be to encourage students to understand the choices they make in the production of particular texts so that they can draw on this information for their own communicative purposes (Bazerman 1988).

Learners need to have an understanding of how features of a situation—such as the participants involved in the communication; the specific purpose(s) of the communication; and a discourse community's values, priorities, and expectations—may impact the choices they make in the production of a particular genre (Johns 1995a). In Thomas Huckin's (1997) view, too much genre analysis has been confined to textual analysis alone. It is important for teachers to be careful that the teaching and learning of genres does not remain the same.

A number of researchers in the new rhetoric have expressed reserva-tions as to whether genres can and should be taught. As a result, their discussions are much less concerned with formal classroom instruction than with the ESP and systemic genre work. For example, Carol Berkenkotter and Thomas Huckin, in their book *Genre Knowledge in Disciplinary Communication* (1995), argue that what we know about genres and appropriate communicative behavior results from our par-ticipation in the activities of daily and professional life, rather than being explicitly taught. In contrast, systemic genre analysts, such as Jennifer Hammond (1987), argue strongly for the explicit teaching of genres, saying that if students are left to work out for themselves how language works, some of them are likely to fail.

It is important to remember that most of the discussion of the teaching and learning of genres in the new rhetoric refers to first, rather than second, language development. As William Grabe and Robert Kaplan (1996) argue, whereas first language students have some implicit knowledge of genres in that language, it is not at all clear that students have the same implicit knowledge with respect to a second language.

Thus, in the view of systemic and ESP genre analysts, descriptions of the discourse structures and language features of genres provide information about genres that is useful for both language teachers and learners. This, of its own, however, is not enough. Genre analysts need to go beyond the text and incorporate ethnographic and informed "insiders' views" into their genre-based descriptions (Tickoo 1994). These genre-based descriptions also need to consider intercultural differences in the realization of different genres. Genre analysis needs to go beyond structural and stylistic examinations of texts to understand more social and contextual features of genres (Swales 1993). Language teachers need to focus on social and contextual features (as much as language features) of genres if they are to provide learners with knowledge (about genres) that will help them achieve their goals.

To summarize, a genre-based approach to language program development aims to incorporate discourse and contextual aspects of language use that are often underattended to in programs based only on lower-level organizational units of language, such as structures, functions, or vocabulary. A genre-based perspective on language program development should not, however, ignore such aspects of language as structures, functions, and vocabulary (Callaghan, Knapp, and Noble 1993). Such aspects of language use are an essential and fundamental part of an effective genre-based language learning program. Nor should it exclude a focus on macro-skills (e.g., reading, writing, listening, and speaking) or specific micro-skills (e.g., reading or listening for gist and working out meaning from context). Rather, such a perspective should focus on such aspects of language use within the social and cultural contexts of the production and interpretation of particular genres. It needs to include a flexible, rather than static, view of genres, one that takes as its starting point the context of production and interpretation of the text, rather than just patterns of organization and linguistic features of the text. When organizational patterns and linguistic features are focused on, they need to be considered in relation to the context and purpose of the genre, participant roles, and the values, traditions, and expectations of the particular discourse community (Johns 1997); that is, genres need to be considered not as patterns of texts in isolation but in relation to the context of production and interpretation and to the aims and assumptions of particular discourse communities. Once students have this understanding, they are better able to choose, for themselves, the strategies they wish to employ to achieve their particular goals.

Benefits of Genre-Based Instruction

One of the aims of a genre-based language learning classroom is the acquisition of what Vijay Bhatia (2000) terms *generic competence,* that is, the ability to participate in and respond to new and recurring genres. This includes the ability to construct, use, and exploit, generic conventions to achieve particular communicative ends. Bhatia (1999a) argues:

> Practicing a genre is almost like playing a game, with its own rules and conventions. Established genre participants . . . are like skilled players, who succeed by their manipulation and exploitation of, rather than a strict compliance with, the rules of the game. . . . It is not simply a matter of learning the language, or even learning the rules of the game, it is more like acquiring the rules of the game in order to be able to exploit and manipulate them to fulfil professional and disciplinary purposes. (25–26)

Generic competence is different from yet includes both linguistic competence and communicative competence; that is, it includes both mastery of the language code (linguistic competence) and the ability to use textual, contextual, and pragmatic knowledge (communicative competence) to both interpret and create contextually appropriate texts as instances of a particular genre (generic competence). Generic competence is not simply about the ability to reproduce discourse forms; it is the ability to understand what happens in real-world interactions and to use this understanding to participate in real-world communicative practices (Bhatia 1999b, 2000).

Clearly, then, genre-based instruction needs to focus on more than just discourse structures and language. To effectively use a genre, students need an understanding of much more than textual features alone. They also need knowledge of the culture, circumstances, purposes, and motives that prevail in particular settings. Participation in a genre means much more than just producing a text that looks like the ones that are usually produced in a particular setting (Dias et al. 1999).

Genre knowledge also includes an understanding of the social and cultural contexts in which genres occur as well as how these factors impact the language choices made within them. Students need to understand the purpose(s) of particular genres as well as the social situation in which they occur (Raimes 1998). Further, as Berkenkotter and Huckin (1995) argue, genre knowledge includes an understanding of what one can appropriately talk or write about in such contexts. This is especially important for language learning classrooms in that many descriptions of genres might focus on the language and structure of a text but pay much less attention to the issue of appropriate content (Connor 1996).

A genre's conventions reveal much about the norms and values of a particular discourse community (Berkenkotter and Huckin 1995). This situated view of genre is clearly highly relevant for language learning classrooms in that it takes us beyond the language and form of a genre to a consideration of the ways in which a genre "is embedded in the communicative activities of the members of a discipline" (Berkenkotter and Huckin 1995, 2). It also gives us insights into the ways people both acquire and use genre knowledge as they participate in different communicative practices.

An important benefit of genre-based instruction is that it helps learners gain access to discourses, texts, and genres that have accrued "cultural capital" in a society (Hammond and Mackin-Horarick 1999). Focusing on genre in language learning classrooms provides a context in which students can gain access to these texts and discourses that will, hopefully, enable them to participate more successfully in spoken and written interactions in a second language. Louise Delpit (1998) argues strongly for teaching these genres, saying that if you are not already a part of the culture of power, "being explicitly told the rules of that culture makes acquiring power easier" (232). In contrast, Alan Luke (1996) argues that learning dominant genres leads to uncritical reproduction of the status quo and does not necessarily provide the kind of access that teachers hope their teaching might provide for their learners. Others argue that not teaching genres of power is socially irresponsible in that already disadvantaged students from non-English-speaking backgrounds are especially disadvantaged by programs that do not address these issues (Christie 1996; Martin 1993). As Hammond and Mackin-Horarick (1999) argue, teaching about genres does not exclude critical analysis of them but provides learners with the necessary base for analyzing and critiquing them.

Smiljka Gee (1997) argues that it is simply sound pedagogic practice to teach learners what they need to know. Acknowledging that the explicit nature of genre-based instruction has been criticized by some, she sees this explicitness as one of its strengths in that it provides a scaffold within which generic components can be placed by learners as needed. Gee argues that a development of genre awareness in terms of types of genre and their characteristic features is essential for learners so that they are aware of the expectations of the context of communication and "the purposes that different genres serve in society and culture" (39).

Genre-based instruction, then, is significantly different from approaches to language teaching that incorporate aspects of language and discourse structure into a lesson but give much less consideration to aspects of the situation, such as role, purpose, content, and communicative expertise required to successfully perform the genre. This is as true of lessons that focus on spoken language as it is of lessons that focus on written language.

A strength of a genre-based syllabus is that it is able to draw together the best aspects of other syllabus models to provide the basis for a coherent, cohesive, and comprehensive framework for language teaching and learning (Feez 1998). A genre-based syllabus incorporates vocabulary and grammatical structures that are typically associated with structural syllabus types; functions and notions that derive from functional-notional approaches to syllabus design; a focus on situation, social activities, and topic that derives from situational and content-based syllabuses; and a focus on specific language learning tasks and activities that draws from task-based and procedural approaches to language teaching and learning. It provides an overarching context, through the notion of genre, for the development of a "mixed syllabus," that is, one that incorporates and draws together features of different syllabus types in a coherent and principled way (Ur 1996). Also, through its focus on whole texts, discourse features of spoken and written texts, and the context of spoken and written interactions, it extends and develops this drawing together of different syllabus types. The notion of genre thus provides a basis for extending current syllabus models, as well as for selecting and sequencing syllabus items and, in turn, focusing on them in the language learning classroom.

In 1996, Sunny Hyon observed that little work at that time had actually investigated the impact of genre-based instruction in the language learning classroom. Some emerging studies suggest that genre-based instruction does have particular benefits. Studies of ESL reading development (e.g., Hewings and Henderson 1987; Hyon 1995; and Raymond 1999) report positive effects of genre instruction on students' understanding of text structure and overall reading effectiveness. Other studies that have examined the effectiveness of genre-based writing instruction show similar gains.

One such study reports on a case study where twenty fifth-grade ESL learners undertook a five-week social studies course that focused on narratives, descriptions, persuasive texts, and expositions (Reppen 1995). The exposition section included compare-and-contrast, problem-solution, and cause-and-effect texts. She found that student writing, content knowledge, and attitudes toward the subject reflected a positive change. In Reppen's view, a genre-based approach offers language learning students valuable practice in valued "ways of writing while also learning content material and working through steps in the writing process." Reppen cautions, however, against turning genre-based instruction into "a formulaic type of instruction in which students are simply instructed to manipulate certain features" (35). Rather, she suggests, students should be encouraged to respond to the content and organizational demands of the various settings in which they find themselves.

A study carried out at the Jordan University of Science and Technology reports similarly positive findings on the effect of genre awareness on linguistic transfer (Mustafa 1995). This study examined the effect of providing ESL students with formal instruction in the conventions of written term papers. The aspects she focused on included the basic parts of a term paper: introduction, body, conclusion, citations, and references. Her study included analysis of students' term papers, student questionnaires, and interviews with professors. She found that her students' writing improved as a result of the instruction, although, interestingly, professors' evaluations of the students' writing seemed to vary in terms of how much they focused on these aspects of the writing in their assessment of the students' work.

A study carried out at the University of Brunei Darussalam, reports positive results of a genre-based academic writing course (Henry and Roseberry 1998). In Australia, an evaluation of the Disadvantaged Schools Project carried out by the National Centre for English Language Teaching and Research in Sydney showed that genre-based instruction had a beneficial impact on student writing (Nunan 1999, 283). To date, most discussions (and evaluations) of genre-based teaching have focused on written language. One of the aims of this book is to show how the notion of genre can be applied as successfully to the teaching and learning of spoken genres as to the teaching and learning of written genres.

Definitions of Genre

Several definitions of the concept of genre as it is used in the area of language teaching and learning have been presented. The *Longman Dictionary of Language Teaching and Applied Linguistics* (Richards, Platt, and Platt 1992) describes genre as a particular class of events that are considered by a discourse community to be the same type. Examples given there are prayers, sermons, conversations, songs, speeches, poems, letters, and novels. Some genres may be called *complex genres* in that a single genre may contain examples of other genres. An example is a church service that contains hymns, psalms, prayers, and a sermon.

John Swales, in his book *Genre Analysis: English in Academic and Research Settings* (1990), proposes a definition of genre that has been extremely influential in the ESP work on genre analysis. A key aspect of this definition is the notion of genre as a class of communicative events with some shared set of communicative purposes. These events may, however, vary in their prototypicality; that is, some instances may be typical examples of the particular genre, whereas others may be less so. The communicative purpose of a particular genre is recognized by members of the discourse community, who, in turn, establish the constraints on what is generally acceptable in terms of content, positioning, and form for a particular genre. Swales also points out that a discourse community's naming of a particular genre gives important insights into genre category membership but typically needs further validation.

From the systemic perspective on genre analysis, Jim Martin (1984) describes genre as "a staged, goal-oriented, purposeful activity in which speakers engage as members of our culture" (25). Genres also have accompanying "schematic" or "generic" structures, that is, typical organizational structures that might include a typical beginning, middle, and end. Thus, genres are staged, culturally purposeful activities that, as Jim Martin argues, users of a language draw on to get things done. Examples of genres examined in this perspective include recounts, procedures, reports, narratives, descriptions, expositions, and observations—that is, descriptions of texts that emphasize the stages through which they move to achieve their particular goal.

Martin (1992) argues that similarities and differences between textual structures provide a means for assigning a text to a particular genre category. Other systemic genre analysts, such as Eija Ventola and Ruqaiya Hasan, also hold this view. Bill Cope and Mary Kalantzis (1993) have critiqued this view of textual structures as being a defining feature of particular genres, pointing out that as more descriptions of genres become available, such a view becomes problematic, especially in situations where a text is, for example, not quite a report, not quite a recount, and not quite a procedure. John Swales (1990) proposes a solution to this problem by drawing on the notions of family resemblances and "sufficient similarity," as well as on work on the notion of prototype. Thus, a text might be considered a "best example" of a particular genre in some cases and an atypical example of the particular genre in others but can still be considered by the discourse community as an instance of the particular genre.

In the new rhetoric, Carolyn Miller (1984) observes that there has not always been firm guidance on how a particular genre might be defined. Among the ways in which this has been attempted, she lists similarities in strategy and form, similarities in audience, similarities in modes of thinking, and similarities in rhetorical situation. She then proposes her own definition of genre, which includes each of these dimensions but takes as its prime focus the action a genre is used to accomplish in a particular, recurring situation. She argues for an open principle for genre classification based in rhetorical practice, rather than a closed one based solely on structure, substance, or "aim" (Miller 1984, 1994).

Thus, there are different views on how to define and identify particular genres. Some hold that a genre can be identified by examination of textual structures alone, and some present the view that genre identification requires a more complex perspective on the notion of genre. The broadest of these views takes the position that several aspects contribute to the identification of a communicative event as an instance of a particular genre and that this cannot necessarily be done with reference to a text's structure alone.

Approaches to Genre Analysis

The main approaches to the analysis of genres in the area of language teaching and learning are the perspective on genre based on the work of John Swales; the approach to genre analysis based on the work of systemic functional linguists, such as Michael Halliday, Ruqaiya Hasan, and Jim Martin; and the perspective on genre based on the work of Carolyn Miller and others in the new rhetoric. There are a number of ways in which these approaches to the descriptions of genres overlap, and ways in which they are quite different from each other. Much of the difference is due to the different goals of each of the approaches to analysis and the differing theoretical positions and concerns that underlie the various approaches.

Both the ESP and the systemic perspectives on genre identify structural elements in texts and make statements about the patterning of these elements. Both, equally, examine the notion of genre-specific language—although they describe this language in rather different terms from each other. ESP genre studies, for example, discuss genre-specific language largely in grammatical terms (e.g., types of verb, noun phrase, and parts of speech), whereas systemic genre studies employ more functional terms (e.g., verbs of action, being, having, or feeling) for their descriptions of genre-specific language.

Discussions of genre in the work of the new rhetoric focus less on features of the text and more on relations between text and context. The relationship between genre and context is also discussed in the systemic view of genre. Here, the relationship is considered in terms of how the "context of culture" and "context of situation" impact textual structures and choices in grammar and vocabulary. Genre studies in the area of ESP also highlight the importance of social and cultural context in their descriptions and explanations of genres, discussing how these impact the language features of a text.

These approaches to the analysis of genres have much in common, with considerable and important overlap among them, even though they deal with very different groups of learners and have, at times, different theoretical concerns (Swales and Hyon 1994; Bloor 1998). There is a need, however, for better articulation among these various perspectives on genre if genre analysis is to realize its potential in the field of language teaching and learning (Atkinson 1996). An important aim of this book will be to illustrate how observations made in each of these perspectives might be drawn together and applied in the language learning classroom.

Tasks and Discussion Questions

1. What is a genre?

a. Group the genres in the following list (from Cook 1989, 95) into categories, such as spoken versus written, degree of formality, purpose of the text, audience of the text. You will see that some genres have things in common but still remain instances of different genres.

recipe	joke	anecdote	label	poem
letter	advertisement	report	message	note
chat	seminar	manifesto	toast	argument
song	novel	notice	biography	sermon
squabble	consultation	sign	essay	jingle

speech	story	article	warrant	ticket
lecture	manual	check	will	conversation
menu	row	prescription	telegram	newspaper

b. Choose one of the genres from the above list and consider it according to the following categories:

1. topic of the text
2. speaker/author of the text
3. audience of the text
4. relationship between participants
5. purpose of the text
6. setting (e.g., in a newspaper, in a classroom, at home)
7. structure of the text
8. tone of the text (e.g., formal vs. informal, serious vs. amusing)
9. patterns of grammar
10. key vocabulary items
11. community expectations
12. shared understandings
13. assumed background knowledge

c. Now find an authentic example of the genre you chose and analyze it according to the above list of categories. Compare your initial analysis with your analysis of an actual text. Which of these features do you think is most helpful in enabling you to categorize the text you examined as an instance of the particular genre? Which of these features would you focus on if you were teaching this genre, and in what order would you focus on them?

2. Definitions of genre

Summarize the main points from the section of this chapter on definitions of genre. Which parts of the definitions do you think are most useful for a language learning classroom? Why?

3. Genre and the notion of prototype

Find several instances of a genre that seem to you to be prototypical of the particular genre. Then find one that is not. How do you think you might deal with this phenomenon in a language learning classroom?

Further Reading

Allison, D. 1999. Key concepts in ELT: Genre. *ELT Journal* 53 (2): 144.

Christie, F. 1999. Genre theory and ESL teaching: A systemic functional perspective. *TESOL Quarterly* 33 (4): 759–63.

Dudley-Evans, T. 1989. An outline of the value of genre analysis in LSP work. In C. Lauren and M. Nordman, eds., *Special Language: From Humans Thinking to Thinking Machines.* Clevedon: Multilingual Matters.

Dudley-Evans, T., and M. J. St. John. 1998. *Developments in English for Special Purposes.* Cambridge: Cambridge University Press. See pp. 87–93, "Discourse and Genre Analysis."

Freedman, A. 1999. Beyond the text: Towards understanding the teaching and learning of genres. *TESOL Quarterly* 33 (4): 764–68.

Freedman, A., and P. Medway, eds. 1994. *Genre and the New Rhetoric.* London: Taylor and Francis. See chapter 1, "Locating Genre Studies: Antecedents and Prospects."

Gee, S. 1997. Teaching writing: A genre-based approach. In G. Fulcher, ed., *Writing in the English Language Classroom.* Hertfordshire, UK: Prentice-Hall Europe ELT.

Grabe, W., and R. Kaplan. 1996. *Theory and Practice of Writing: An Applied Linguistic Perspective.* London: Longman. See chapter 5, pp. 133–40, "Genre-Based Approaches to Writing Development."

Jordan, R. R. 1997. *English for Academic Purposes: A Guide and Resource Book for Teachers.* Cambridge: Cambridge University Press. See pp. 230–40, "Genre Analysis"; pp. 240–43.

Kay, H., and T. Dudley-Evans. 1998. Genre: What teachers think. *ELT Journal* 52 (4): 308–14.

McCarthy, M., and R. Carter. 1994. *Language as Discourse: Perspectives for Language Teaching.* London: Longman. See chapter 1.6, pp. 24–38, "Genres."

Swales, J. M. 1986. A genre-based approach to language across the curriculum. In M. L. Tickoo, ed., *Language across the Curriculum.* Anthology Series, no. 15. Singapore: SEAMEO Regional Language Centre.

Swales, J. M. 1990. *Genre Analysis: English in Academic and Research Settings.* Cambridge: Cambridge University Press. See chapter 3, "The Concept of Genre."

Chapter 2

Genre and the Language Learning Classroom

Classroom applications of genre studies have taken place in different ways in different parts of the world. They have also had different underlying goals and focused on different teaching situations. Systemic classroom applications in Australia, for example, have had a different ideological focus from ESP and new rhetoric genre work, in part because of the Australian work's underlying concern with "empowering" underprivileged learners and providing them with the language resources that are necessary for success.

ESP applications have been mostly concerned with the teaching of international students in English-medium universities in Britain and abroad. Here, the focus has been less on "empowerment" and more on "demystifying" the use of English in academic contexts and providing students with the language resources and skills that will help them gain access to English-language academic discourse communities.

North American new rhetoric studies have been principally geared toward a more academic audience than has the ESP and systemic classroom-based work. The main focus of new rhetoric discussions is on mainstream, native speaker students and professionals rather than language learners. Much of the new rhetoric genre work also assumes a certain familiarity with work in such areas as composition studies and rhetoric and has presented much less in the way of educational guidelines than have the other two perspectives (Hyon 1995). Many academic texts in the area of ESP and systemic genre studies have assumed a similar level of audience to that of the new rhetoric genre work. The results of these analyses, however, have been transferred more into classroom-based materials written in a way that is accessible to teachers who do not have a theoretical background in the particular framework the materials draw on for their analyses.

The new rhetoric has not, however, ignored practical implications of its theoretical discussions. Charles Bazerman (1988), for example, discusses "writing well" from a scientific and rhetorical point of view, focusing on such areas as the assumptions and goals of the text and the writer's "place" in the discourse community. Richard Coe (1994) describes raising students' awareness of the social contexts that shape their writing, by asking them to specify the purpose, audience, and circumstances of their writing text and then assess their texts in relation to these factors. Graeme Smart (1992) describes how his ethnographic investigations into the production and expectations of "bank genres" have helped inform his teaching of them. Patrick Dias and his colleagues (Dias et al. 1999) examine the relationship between writing in (native speaker) university courses and writing in parallel workplace settings, finding that these locations are "worlds apart" (the title of their book) from each other.

Examples of course books based on the ESP view of genre include Tony Dudley-Evans's *Writing Laboratory Reports* (1985), Robert Weissberg and Suzanne Buker's *Writing Up Research: Experimental Report Writing for Students of English* (1990), and John Swales and Christine Feak's *Academic Writing for Graduate Students: Essential Tasks and Skills* (1994) and *English in Today's Research World: A Writing Guide* (2000).

In the area of ESP, a distinction is sometimes made between "common-core" and "specific" approaches to the teaching of English in academic contexts. Tony Dudley-Evans (1995b) describes a program in which both of these approaches are taken into account. This involves common-core teaching of general academic language, as well as specific classes that focus on the assignment requirements of specific departments. The common-core component of the program teaches general discourse-level conventions and typical patterns of grammar and vocabulary found (in this case) in theses and research reports. The subject-specific classes are team taught by a subject specialist and a language teacher. These classes include discussion of the strategies and language that are appropriate to subject-specific tasks required in the particular course the students are taking. The program thus focuses on the "general expectations" of the genres students need to write and the "particular expectations" of the subject area or discipline in which the genres are being written.

Also in the area of ESP, John Flowerdew (1993) argues for a procedure that focuses on the process of learning about and acquiring genres, rather than one that focuses solely on the end product, or specific variety of genre. A similar argument is presented by Badger and

White (2000), who say that process and product approaches to genre-based teaching should be thought of as being complementary rather than in opposition to each other (see Raimes 1991 for a similar argument).

Flowerdew argues for an educational rather than a training approach to the teaching and learning of genres. He argues that teachers cannot always predict the range of genres in which students will need to be able to participate. In his view, teachers need to help learners see how they can go about discovering how genres differ from one another and how the same genre may vary. Flowerdew questions the rigid way in which genres are sometimes presented in the language learning classroom, making the important point that models of genres presented in the classroom should be treated not as fixed, rule-governed patterns but as prototypes that allow for individual variation.

John Swales's work in the area of genre analysis has always had a strong pedagogical focus, right from his early work on genre analysis. His coauthored text on academic writing for graduate students (Swales and Feak 1994) is, in many ways, a drawing together of much of his work in this area. John Swales and Christine Feak avoid laying down "rules" for what a student should and should not write in a particular situation. Rather, they encourage students to explore, for themselves, exactly what the particular expectations of their discipline might be.

Systemic genre-based applications initially focused on writing in Australian primary and secondary schools. More recently, they have also been applied in adult migrant ESL settings, in English-in-the-workplace programs, and to ESL writing in university settings. The systemic approach emphasizes the importance of teaching language at the discourse, or whole text, level, rather than restricting it to the sentence level. The teaching of grammar and vocabulary, for example, in systemic genre-based classrooms is undertaken in conjunction with the teaching of whole texts. This approach stresses the central role of context and the way in which language changes and is changed by the contexts in which it occurs. Classroom applications of the systemic perspective thus focus on text and context and discuss in relation to them such aspects of language as discourse, vocabulary, grammar, and pronunciation (Burns and Joyce 1997).

The systemic perspective on genre has been taken up, in particular, in New South Wales Adult Migrant English Service (AMES) programs for adult ESL learners. The systemic perspective on genre is also one of the key theoretical underpinnings of the New South Wales AMES *Certificate in Written and Spoken English,* a national curriculum document developed by a project team from the Curriculum Support Unit of the New South Wales AMES (Hagan et al. 1993).

The systemic perspective on genre has also influenced other curriculum guidelines published by the New South Wales AMES, such as Susan Cornish's *Community Access: Curriculum Guidelines* (1992), as well as more general books for language teachers, such as Helen Joyce's *Workplace Texts in the Language Classroom* (1992) and Jennifer Hammond and colleagues's *English for Social Purposes. A Handbook for Teachers of Adult Literacy* (Hammond et al. 1992), the latter produced by the National Centre for English Language Teaching and Research at Macquarie University in Sydney.

Genre as an Organizing Principle for Language Learning Programs

A number of authors have discussed the notion of genre as an organizing principle for language learning programs. In the area of ESP, Florence Davies (1988) describes an academic English genre-based syllabus that is integrated with a reading syllabus. The focus of her course is the specific genres that university students are required to read and write in their subject-based studies. She is particularly interested in what Swales (1996) calls *occluded genres,* that is, genres that can be difficult for students to access or study, such as exam answers, essays, laboratory reports, dissertations, and theses. She points out, however, that a genre-based syllabus needs to involve teacher and student collaboration in the identification of target genres and tasks if it is to achieve its aims and be relevant to the students' interests and needs.

A genre-based syllabus need not contain a set of preselected texts (Bhatia 1993). Rather, it can contain a list of genres and task types that then can be designed around specific texts. The final selection of texts for use in the classroom can be left to the teacher and students to decide, depending on their particular interest, motivation, and purpose.

The choice of appropriate tasks in a genre-based language learning program is especially important. The texts chosen for study and the tasks chosen to examine them need to be interrelated; that is, the tasks need to focus directly on the particular genre skills that the program is aiming to achieve (Swales 1990). An analysis of the genres students need to acquire and the actual purpose to which they are put needs to provide the basis for these tasks; tasks should not be selected in isolation from the particular genres.

The New South Wales AMES *Certificate in Spoken and Written English* (Hagan et al. 1993) provides descriptions of three stages of English language proficiency (beginner, postbeginner, and intermediate) as well as competency descriptions for English for study purposes, vocational English, and English for community access. These descriptions include consideration of the purpose of the genre, the discourse structure, and such aspects of language as grammar, vocabulary, graphology, and phonology. Table 1 presents a description of a student's ability to negotiate a simple oral transaction to obtain specific goods and services.

Burns and Joyce (1997) describe the basic stages of designing a genre-based course.

1. Identify the overall context of language use.
2. Develop goals or aims.
3. Note the sequence of language events within the particular context.
4. List the genres arising from this sequence.
5. Outline the sociocultural knowledge that students need in the particular communicative context.
6. Record or gather samples of the genres on which the course will focus.
7. Develop units of work related to these genres and develop the learning objectives to be achieved.

Table 2 provides an example of the application of this framework to a course that focuses on preparing students for university study. The genres shown in bold highlight the spoken genres students require in this particular context. Written genres are shown in normal print. This kind of task is based on what is referred to in the ESP literature as a *target situation analysis* of students' language learning needs (Robinson 1991, 8).

It is also important to establish learners' individual language learning needs in a genre-based language learning program. This is sometimes referred to as a *present situation analysis* (Robinson 1991, 9). This might be done by carrying out individual student interviews, group discussions, and self-assessment tasks or by means of surveys or questionnaires. Other information should include the results of tests that ask students to perform target-level tasks and any available precourse information on the students' language learning backgrounds, proficiency, and strengths and weaknesses. The process of observing and diagnosing the learners' needs should continue throughout the course. This information can then be used to modify course objectives and to intervene as appropriate in the course of the language learning program.

TABLE 1. A Competency Statement: Can Negotiate a Simple Oral Transaction to Obtain Specific Goods and Services

Elements	Performance Criteria	Range of Variables	Examples of Texts/ Assessment Tasks
Purpose i. has knowledge of purpose of text to obtain goods/ services in a short spoken exchange	• successful transaction achieved	• familiar/relevant subject matter	**Texts** • Shopping exchanges • Public transport service encounter
Discourse Structure ii. has knowledge of appropriate staging of text iii. can request desired goods/service and respond with relevant information iv. can manage some conversational techniques (verbally or nonverbally)	• produces appropriate opening and closing stages of transaction • requests desired goods/service and responds appropriately with relevant information • uses minimal conversational techniques to check, clarify; asks for repetition verbally or nonverbally— relies on gesture as required	• can rely on gesture to support the exchange • interlocutor has experience with NESB speakers • recourse to repetition/ clarification	
Grammar/Vocabulary v. can understand an use common greetings, courtesy expressions, and formulaic expressions vi. can use key vocabulary and grammatical forms	• uses some common greetings, courtesy expressions, and formulaic expressions • uses key vocabulary and some grammatical forms, e.g., desired shopping items, travel destinations, simple questions may use lexical items only and/or limited range of grammatical structures	• short utterances only— long pauses and hesitation by speaker acceptable	**Tasks** • Role play—buy a weekly ticket • Role play—make an appointment to see the doctor • Role play—learner buys stamps from post office • Role play—basic enquiry about a job vacancy
Phonology vii. can produce recognizable pronunciation and stress/ intonation patterns	• produces most intelligible pronunciation/stress/ intonation, which may require interlocutor to verify		

Source: From Hagan et al. 1993, 19.

TABLE 2. Designing a Course for Students Preparing to Study at a University

Step	Discussion and Examples
1. **Identify the overall context**	University: course focus is preparing students for study at university
2. **Develop an aim**	To develop the spoken and written language skills required to undertake university study
3. **Note the language event sequence within the context**	These could include: • **enrolling at university** • **discussing course selection** • **attending lectures** • **attendng tutorials** • **using the library** • reading reference books • writing essays • writing reports • undertaking examinations • **participating in casual conversations**
4. **List the texts arising from the sequence**	These could include: • enrollment forms • **service encounter—selecting courses** • **lectures** • **tutorial discussions** • **service encounter—library enquiry** • Range of possible written texts, for example: —discipline-specific essays —discipline-specific reports • Range of possible reading texts, for example: —discipline-specific journal articles —discipline-specific books —library catalogues —lecture notes • examination papers • **genres within casual conversation (e.g., anecdote)**
5. **Outline the sociocultural knowledge students need**	Students need knowledge about: • academic institutions • academic procedures and expectations • the role of the student
6. **Record or gather samples of texts**	• Written texts: Gather examples of essays, catalogues, journals, etc. • Spoken texts: You may need to: —find available recordings —prepare some semi-scripted dialogues yourself —record authentic interactions
7. **Develop units of work related to the texts and develop learning objectives to be achieved**	Classroom tasks should be sequenced within units of work to provide students with: • explicit input • guided practice • an opportunity to perform independently

Source: From Burns and Joyce 1997, 79.

The extent to which teachers are able to make decisions about what they will teach and how they will teach it often depends on the teaching situation (Burns and Joyce 1997). In some situations, the content of the course is predetermined either by an in-house syllabus or by a course book that needs to be followed. In other situations, the teacher might have complete freedom in the development of the teaching program. The curriculum framework of the *Certificate in Spoken and Written English* lies between these two positions in that the overall genres and aims of the program are specified but the teacher is able to choose the texts and contexts through which the outcomes specified in the framework will be achieved.

An Example from the Classroom

Described here is a genre-based English language program for first-year ESL students studying in an English-language academic learning environment. The program focuses on the development of key academic genres and provides an opportunity for the development of personal language and learning skills. The program also integrates process- and product-oriented approaches to language program design with content-based approaches to the teaching of academic writing, by drawing on Ann Raimes's (1991) notion of a balanced process approach to language program development that pays attention to form, content, and reader expectations along with focussing on the individual writer.

The specific aims of the program are to develop the students' abilities

- to read and extract information from a range of genres relevant to the gathering of information for academic purposes
- to write and speak a range of genres and text types that meet the demands and expectations of an English-medium academic learning environment
- to recognize required genres and text types in assessment and evaluation procedures and to create appropriate responses to questions

The content in which learning tasks are embedded includes such topics as English as an international language, native and nonnative varieties of English, implications for international and intercultural communication, and the influence of English on other languages. This thematic approach is supported by research into the effect of subject-matter knowledge and its impact on writing performance, which has found that the extent to which ESL writers are familiar with subject matter has dramatic influences on their writing performance (Tedick 1990). It is also supported by studies that have concluded that academic skills are best taught in connection with authentic content material (Adamson 1990).

The course further reflects an integrated approach to language use in that students develop their ability to transfer from one mode of language use to another in a way that reflects the language behavior and expectations of an English-language academic learning environment. For example, students read and discuss texts on related topics for the creation of pieces of written work and in preparation for examination on the particular topic. The course thus aims to approximate actual conditions of language use in an academic context.

Writing tasks focused on in the program aim to cover the range of basic writing requirements of an English-medium academic learning environment. These include summaries of or reactions to readings, annotated bibliographies, reports, case studies, documented essays, and research projects. Text types focused on in these pieces of writing include problem-solution, topic/restriction/illustration, description, discussion, cause-and-effect, and compare-and-contrast texts. Spoken genres concentrate largely on seminar presentations and tutorial discussion, both genres that have been described in the literature as being particularly problematic for students from non-English-speaking backgrounds. Examples of written assignments, topic areas, genres, and text types focused on in the program are shown in table 3.

The program also includes preparation for an end-of-course examination that covers the major content areas of the course. In analyzing and responding to the examination questions, students are required to answer long- and short-answer questions and to draw on skills developed in the course. Particular attention is given in this preparation to the analysis of examination prompts and identification of required text types.

In the area of writing, the program focuses on reader expectations and the stages of the writing process. Learners engage in planning, drafting, reviewing, revising, and editing their work as they work toward approximating models of the various types of writing required of them in an academic learning environment. Work on spoken genres includes classroom discussion of the role and purpose of seminar presentations and tutorials, characteristics of spoken versus written language, and observation and analysis of real-life examples of the particular genres.

TABLE 3. A Genre-Based Academic English Program: Examples of Written Assignments, Topic Areas, Genres, and Text Types.

Topic Area	Assignment Tasks	Genre and Text Type
English as an International Language	What is English as an International Language? What problems arise when English is used as an international language and what can be done to help solve them?	Documented essay (description/compare and contrast/problem-solution)
What English for second language learners?	Yukawa 1989 argues that it is not necessary for second language learners to match native-English-speaking linguistic and sociolinguistic abilities. What do you think should be the linguistic and sociolinguistic goals of second language learners of English. Why?	Documented essay (argument)
World Englishes	What are World Englishes? Look at the references given by Kachru (1989) and summarize several key readings on the subject. Be sure to include examples of World Englishes as well as examples of how English is used in the world and the people that use it.	Summary of readings (description)
Attitude toward English	Prepare and carry out a study of your fellow students' attitudes towards Egnlish. Focus, in particular, on their reasons for studying English and their opinions regarding different varieties of English.	Report (discussion)
Intercultural communication	Identify a collection of key books or articles on the subject of intercultural communication and write an annotated bibliography of these readings.	Annotated bibliography (description)
Communication strategies	Observe a fellow student in this course over a period of several weeks and identify the communication strategies s/he uses when speaking English. Discuss your observations with the student, then compare the results of your study with those of Tarone and Yule (1987).	Case study (compare and contrast)
The effect of English on other languages	Look at a particular topic in a newspaper, journal, or magazine in a language other than English over a regular period. What borrowings from English can you find? Use these examples to discuss how and why languages change.	Research project (cause and effect)

Source: From Paltridge 1995c.

Systems of Genres and the Language Learning Classroom

Often, only certain genres may appropriately follow other genres. Also, one genre is often dependent on the outcome of another genre. For example, a call to a job interview is dependent on an applicant having been selected for interview and (normally) having made a formal application for the position. This sequence of genres may be highly constrained in some circumstances, such as with the law, and less so in others. Nonetheless, teachers (and our students) need to be able to perform each of the genres well when the appropriate occasion arises (Bazerman 1994).

Business English students often say they need to learn how to have dinner-party conversations, how to order a drink in a bar, how to order a meal in a restaurant (for themselves and for someone else), the rules of interaction at a dinner table (e.g., who pours a drink for whom and how it is done), and how to "keep a conversation going." Much business is done while taking part in these kinds of genre. Moreover, the results of our participation in these genres often interact in various ways with what we might do and say in other genres, such as memos, reports, and business presentations.

Conversation skills are also important for EAP students, who need to be able to interrupt, disagree, and talk about nonconcrete topics as much as they need academic listening, reading, and writing skills. It is thus important for teachers to remember that systems of genres include both spoken and written genres, even though the final focus may be on a written or spoken genre alone. As Berkenkotter and Huckin (1995) point out, genre knowledge is constructed as much through conversations with peers and colleagues as through written texts.

Teachers also need to remember that genre knowledge includes knowledge of appropriate content (Berkenkotter and Huckin 1995). For example, a student needs to know not only how to have a dinner party conversation or how to write a letter of application but also what it is important and appropriate to talk (or write) about in such settings.

Investigating Systems of Genres

Students can be given tasks that ask them to work out the place of the particular genre they are studying in its particular genre system. Teachers and curriculum designers also need to carry out their own investigations that incorporate the notion of systems of genres. This can include observations, interviews, and teacher introspections to predict and identify related genres. It is important to remember, however, that such information sources as interviews and introspections may give idealized versions of what people do rather than what they actually do. It is important, then, to combine such information with observations and collections of real texts, whenever possible.

Cross-Cultural Comparisons

It is also helpful to ask students to consider particular genre systems in their first language. They can then do cross-cultural comparisons of systems of genres to see what is the same and what is different in English and in their first language. They can also compare differing assumptions and expectations between the genre systems in the two languages and cultures. For example, when applying for certain jobs in Italy, it is often helpful to have someone who knows you and can "put in a word for you" (called, in Italian, a *raccomandazione*) when you apply for the position. Some public positions in Italy, including very senior ones, also require the applicant to take part in a public written examination, or *concorso,* which occurs much less often in English-speaking contexts. Thus, systems of genres may include certain genres and interactions in some cultures but not in others.

Event Sequences

Anne Burns, Helen Joyce, and Sandra Gollin, in their book *I See What You Mean: Using Spoken Discourse in the Classroom* (1996), give examples of event sequences (Hood, Solomon, and Burns 1995) that are helpful for considering the notion of systems of genres in language learning classrooms. Figure 1 shows a possible sequence of events for medical consultations in Australia. This sequence clearly may vary between surgeries and in different parts of Australia. Research has shown, further, that this particular event sequence may be quite different in other countries (see, e.g., Ranney 1992). It is helpful, nonetheless, as an indication of the genres students need to be familiar with beyond the central medical consultation itself, as well as an indication of the typical event sequence with which students need to be familiar.

Students need to know much more than just grammar, vocabulary, and formulaic phrases to operate successfully in such contexts (Burns, Joyce, and Gollin 1996). They also need knowledge of how whole texts operate and interact with each other and of particular social and

1. Telephone the doctor's surgery to make an appointment	2. Report to the doctor's receptionist	3. Engage in the medical consultation	4. Obtain a prescription
5. Take the prescription to a pharmacist	6. Engage in a service encounter	7. Read the instructions on the medication	8. Complete a form to claim a government refund of part of the doctor's fee

Fig. 1. An event sequence: A typical medical consultation in Australia. (Adapted from Burns, Joyce, and Gollin 1996, 35.)

and cultural practices. This might include an understanding of particular event sequences, or systems of genres, or it might include an understanding of particular "sets" of genres (Swales 2000a)—that is, collections of genres that are in a relationship with each other but in less of a linear arrangement, such as academic essays, which may interact with other genres but in a range of different possible orders.

In other settings, students might have a range of choices of genres to achieve a particular goal; that is, they might choose from a "repertoire" of genres (Swales 2000a). For example, to find out a particular piece of information, a person might use an E-mail message, a phone call, a fax, a letter, or a conversational genre, according to the particular situation.

Communication Networks

A helpful way of drawing on the notion of systems, or sets, of genres is through the use of *communication networks* (Nunan and Burton 1989; Burns, Joyce, and Gollin 1996). Communication networks can be used to identify the contexts in which students need to interact, the people students need to interact with, and the genres students need to control. The networks can be completed by the students themselves or jointly with the teacher. The networks can also be used with people students interact with outside the classroom, to provide information on the genres students need to command. Once the students' genre needs are established, the network can be used as the basis for planning particular units of work and event sequences for classroom focus (Burns, Joyce, and Gollin 1996). Figure 2 is an example of a communication network

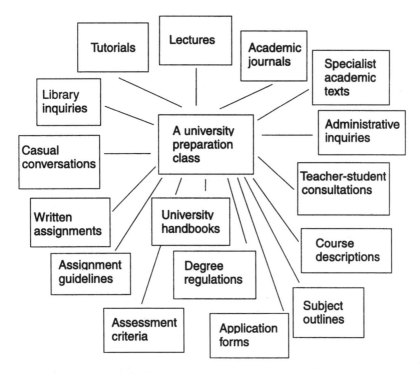

Fig. 2. A communication network: A university preparation class. (Adapted from Burns, Joyce, and Gollin 1996, 79.)

based on the genres with which students preparing to study at a college or university need to be familiar.

Once a genre has been selected for focus, samples of the genre, if available, can be collected, analyzed, transcribed (in the case of spoken texts), and used as the basis for developing in-class and out-of-class tasks that focus on the particular genre (Burns, Joyce, and Gollin 1996). The analysis of the sample texts might consider aspects of the genre and situation in which it occurs, such as

- the social and cultural context of the genre
- the purpose of the genre
- the content of the genre
- the writer or speaker of the genre
- the intended audience for the particular genre
- the relationships between participants in the genre
- the setting of the genre (e.g., in a newspaper, in a classroom, at home)
- the structure of the genre

- the tone of the genre (e.g., formal vs. informal, serious vs. amusing)
- discourse community expectations
- shared understandings between participants
- assumed background knowledge
- key vocabulary items
- typical patterns of grammar
- the relationships the genre has with other genres, including its place in any event sequence it might be part of

When the learning tasks have been carried out, they can be reviewed and discussed with the class, then any necessary reteaching or further development work can be undertaken. This procedure can then recommence with other genres within the particular system of genres, at whatever stage is appropriate to the learners' needs (Burns, Joyce, and Gollin 1996).

The notion of systems of genres is an important aspect of genre knowledge "outside the text" and can be usefully explored in the language learning classroom. As Ann Johns (1991) has observed, there is sometimes a tendency for teachers and curriculum designers to intuit the needs and future language uses of students, rather than to attempt to discover them. The notion of systems of genres, combined with descriptions of event sequences and communication networks, can provide one way in which teachers can examine the tasks students need to perform in English and the target situations in which students need to operate, so that teachers can make descriptions of genres pedagogically more useful and relevant to the needs of learners.

A Teaching and Learning Cycle

Many systemic-oriented genre-based textbooks discuss a particular teaching and learning cycle that is often associated with systemic classroom applications. This teaching and learning cycle is reproduced in figure 3. The teaching and learning cycle aims to provide support for learners as they move from building up the content of a text, through the presentation and discussion of a model of the target text, to a "joint construction" (by the teacher and learners) of a further model text. At each of these stages, learners' attention is drawn to the cultural and social context of the text, the structure of the text, the content of the text, and characteristic linguistic features of the text. The teacher may enter at any phase of the cycle, depending on the learner's stage of preparedness for

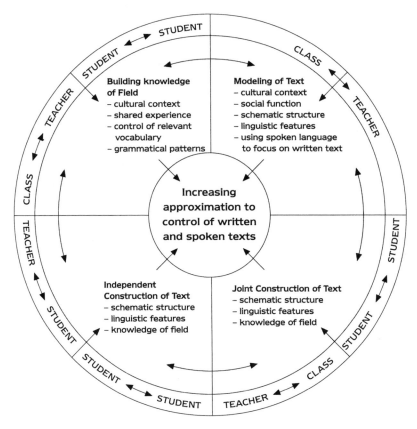

Fig. 3. The systemic teaching and learning cycle. (From Hammond et al. 1992, 17.)

the particular activity; that is, the cycle is intended to be used flexibly, with teachers encouraged to enter the cycle at whatever point best meets their students' needs (Hammond et al. 1992).

This teaching and learning cycle is based on the notion of *scaffolding* (Bruner 1975; Wood, Bruner, and Ross 1976; Cazden 1988), which draws from Vygotsky's (1978) view that higher thinking processes, including language, arise as a consequence of human interaction. Scaffolding involves providing support for learners as they develop in their linguistic competence. Integral to this notion is the idea that learners are "in the position of solving a problem that is beyond their level of competence" (Hawkins 1988, 2). At the same time, the person that is helping them is in the position of "knowing" how to perform the task. Through the scaffolded interaction, learners come to the point where they are able to perform the task, first with assistance, then independently (Hawkins 1988).

A classroom activity may typically commence with "high teacher scaffolding," where students are dependent on the teacher for input and explicit instruction. Scaffolding might be provided in relation to cultural, social, contextual, and linguistic information associated with the particular genre being studied. It might also include the presentation of a model of the genre, which may focus on the structure of the genre and typical vocabulary and grammatical choices. Scaffolding might also be provided in the explanation and modeling of classroom tasks, so that students are aware of what is required of them in the language learning activities. Once students' competence increases, the teacher focuses less on input and instruction and begins to act as a facilitator for classroom activities. This includes encouraging students to communicate, monitoring their performance, and providing feedback on their work. Learners move toward their own independent performance of a task through the "assisted performance" (Tharp and Gallimore 1991) of an "expert."

This approach is similar in many ways to what Evelyn Hatch (1986) terms the "experience" model of language learning. Hatch discusses how, in interactions with more expert language users, learners are able to build and refine knowledge structures for conversational interactions. These knowledge structures might include information about conversational openings, closings, and the turn-taking system, as well as particular linguistic items. As new information is encountered, she argues, new information is checked against old information, and the knowledge structures become progressively more refined, reorganized, and efficient. In the language learning classroom, this learning is guided via learners' interactions with their teacher or other more expert learners who either explicitly or implicitly provide them with information about preferred discourse structures and relevant linguistic features in their interactions.

Barbara Hawkins (1988) provides examples of how second language learners, through scaffolded classroom interactions, are capable of higher-level cognitive activities than they would have been on their own. She also shows how scaffolded interactions lead to improved language learning and the development of associated problem-solving skills. She points out that scaffolding is more likely to be effective when the situation is both interactively and cognitively demanding for students and when there is a real reason for interaction—that is, where there is a genuine level of information exchange between the teacher and the learners or between the learners themselves. These kinds of scaffolded interaction, Hawkins argues, provide "abundant opportunities for linguistic and cognitive modeling and development" (128), and although it may take more time for a teacher to scaffold, there is evidence that it is time well spent.

Other, more recent research has shown similar gains through scaffolded classroom interactions. It has shown, in particular, how language learners are able to reach higher levels of performance by working together and providing assistance to one another than they might have achieved by working on their own (see, e.g., Kowal and Swain 1994; Donato 2000; Ohta 2000).

Activity types that might be drawn on in a scaffolded teaching and learning cycle include:

- Preparation activities
- Activities that focus on discourse awareness and skills
- Activities that focus on language awareness and skills
- Language practice activities
- Extension activities

(Burns and Joyce 1997)

These activities can be used in any particular order, depending on student needs. Detailed examples of each kind of activity are presented in the chapters that follow.

Genre, Conversation, and the Language Learning Classroom

There are different views in the literature of genre analysis as to whether conversation should be treated as a genre in language learning classrooms. John Swales (1990), for example, calls conversation a "pre-genre," saying that ordinary conversation is too fundamental to be usefully considered a genre. Conversations do, however, have many particular characteristics, such as ways of opening and closing, culture specific rules, and conventions for turn taking, as well as various strategies for holding on to a turn, for changing a topic, and for correcting what was said. Conversations also have a number of event-specific purposes and typical schematic structures, as research into the nature of casual conversations is beginning to show.

Suzanne Eggins and Diana Slade, in their book *Analysing Casual Conversation* (1997), present a view of casual conversation that is useful for the language learning classroom and that has important implications for genre-based teaching. They argue that casual conversations are used to negotiate social identity and interpersonal relations, whereas such interactions as service encounters or university lectures perform quite different, pragmatic tasks. They also argue that casual conversation is extremely important and needs to be taught.

From a teaching point of view, then, there are certain advantages in taking casual conversation to be a genre, that is, "a staged, goal-oriented purposeful activity" (Martin 1984, 25) that speakers of a language use to accomplish particular social and cultural goals. In particular, it gives learners a context for language use (and teachers a context for instruction) in which they may give attention to many contextual and discourse-level aspects of spoken language that are not often focused on in language learning classrooms. Clearly, many features of casual conversation occur within the context of other spoken genres as well. The same could be said, however, for grammar and vocabulary, which, even though they may be focused on within the context of a particular genre, also occur within the context of many other genres.

Language teaching has tended to regard casual conversation as unstructured and therefore unteachable in any explicit sense (Eggins and Slade 1997). Eggins and Slade argue that this is not the case and that explicit features of casual conversation can and should be taught. In their view, without the ability to participate in casual conversations, second language learners are destined to remain excluded from social intimacy with speakers of the target language and will therefore be denied the benefits of full participation in the cultural life of English-speaking countries.

Rob Nolasco and Lois Arthur, in their book *Conversation* (1987), equally argue for a focus on casual conversation in language learning classrooms, pointing out that language teachers often tend to assume that conversation involves nothing more than putting into practice the grammar and vocabulary skills taught elsewhere in the course. They argue, also, that teachers need to teach what native speakers of language "do" when they have conversations and to develop appropriate classroom materials and techniques that focus on this particular context of language use.

Teaching casual conversation as a genre, then, provides opportunities for focusing on discourse-level aspects of spoken interactions that are very often not attended to in language learning classrooms. Discourse structure is, however, generally less easy to predict in conversations than in many other genres. For example, conversations tend to be more open-ended and to involve more shifts in topic than is the case with some other genres. Generally, however, there are many aspects of conversation that typically occur and that can be usefully focused on in the language learning classroom.

Openings and Closings

Openings and closings in conversations are often carried out in typical ways. They often make use of pairs of utterances, or *adjacency pairs,* which may perform a ritual function in the conversation rather than being taken literally. For example:

A: Hi.
B: How're you doing?

and

A: Bye.
B: See you later.

Further, closings are often preceded by *preclosings* accompanied by falling intonation, such as

Okay
Good
Well, I'd better go now
Anyway, it's been nice talking to you
Anyhow, thanks for calling

These kinds of conversational strategy vary, however, from culture to culture. Just because a learner is able to open and close a conversation in his or her first language does not mean that he or she will know how to do this in another language. Conversational openings and closings therefore benefit from being focused on in the language learning classroom.

Schematic Structures

Between these beginnings and endings, conversations may have different internal schematic structures. Eggins and Slade (1997)—after the work of Labov and Waletzky (1967), Plum (1988), Rothery (1990), Martin (1992), and Horvarth and Eggins (1995)—give examples of narrative, anecdote, recount, and opinion texts within the context of conversational interactions. They observe that other types of conversation, such as chat, typically have more open and less identifiable internal structures. The schematic structures they observe are shown below. (See Burns, Joyce, and Gollin 1996; Carter and McCarthy 1997; Eggins and Slade 1997 for examples of these kinds of conversations.) Parentheses indicate that a stage is optional; that is, it may or may not occur in the conversation.

Narrative

1. (Abstract)
2. (Orientation)
3. Complication
4. Evaluation
5. Resolution
6. (Coda)

Anecdote

1. (Abstract)
2. (Orientation)
3. Remarkable event
4. Reaction
5. (Coda)

Recount

1. (Abstract)
2. Orientation
3. Record of events
4. (Coda)

Opinion

1. Opinion
2. Reaction
3. (Evidence)
4. (Resolution)

Turn Taking

Different languages have different norms and conventions for who talks, when, and for how long. In English, one person normally speaks at a time. When someone has finished speaking, he or she may nominate another speaker, or another speaker may simply take the turn without being nominated. There are a number of ways in which English speakers signal that they have come to the end of a turn. For example, they may complete a syntactic unit then pause. They may signal the end of a turn by using falling intonation with such items as "mhm," "so," or "anyway." They might also use eye contact, body position and movement, or low pitch to indicate the end of a turn.

English speakers also use particular strategies to hold on to a turn. For example, they might avoid pausing too long at the end of a sentence and start straight away on another one. An English speaker might also hold on to a turn by pausing in the middle of what he or she is saying; by using fillers, such as "ahhh" and "ummm," while searching for a word; by increasing the volume of what he or she is saying; or by "speaking over" someone else who attempts to take the turn.

Native speakers normally find it relatively easy and natural to know who is to speak, when, and for how long (Nolasco and Arthur 1987). This skill is not, however, automatically transferred to another language. Many language learners "have great difficulty in getting into a conversation, knowing when to give up their turn to others, and in bringing a conversation to a close" (Nolasco and Arthur 1987, 9–10). We need to train learners to sense when someone is about to finish a turn, how they can signal this to someone else, and how they can take a turn in a conversation.

Adjacency Pairs

We often rely on adjacency pairs to communicate what we want to say and to interpret what other people are saying. Adjacency pairs are pairs of utterances that typically occur in a particular sequence. In the following example from a late-night radio talk show, a caller phones to dedicate a song to her boyfriend. After the announcer's opening address to his audience, the rest of the conversation continues in sets of adjacency pairs, with the first utterance in each pair being matched by an "expected follow-up."

> *A:* Sharon Stone's on the line.
>   How are you?
> *B:* Really good.
> *A:* I bet you get hassled about your name.
> *B:* Yes, I do.

A: And what would you like to tell Patrick?

B: Ummm . . . that I love him very much and that I wish him a very happy birthday for today.

The basic rule for adjacency pairs, which both of these speakers follow, is that when someone produces the first part of a pair, he or she should stop talking and allow the other person to produce a second part. There is, however, a certain amount of freedom in responding to some first parts of adjacency pairs. Some second parts may be *preferred,* and others may be *dispreferred.* For example, when the first part of a pair is an *invitation,* the preferred second part would be an *accept;* the dispreferred second part would be a *reject.* When someone provides a dispreferred second part, it is often preceded by a *delay,* a *preface,* and/or an *account.* For example:

A: Would you like to come for a drink after work? (invitation)

B: Uhhh (delay) . . . I'd really like to (preface), but I've still got a lot of work to finish (account). Can we make it another night? (reject)

Sometimes speakers use *insertion sequences* between adjacency pairs; that is, they place one adjacency pair between the first and second parts of another adjacency pair. In the following example of someone ordering food in a restaurant, the customer uses an insertion sequence to check on one of the dishes before ordering.

A: What would you like?

B: Is the chicken curry really hot?

A: No, it's quite mild.

B: Okay, I'll have the chicken curry, and my wife would like the fresh vegetables and tofu.

Topic Management

Topic management is another important aspect of casual conversation that can be usefully focused on in a language learning classroom. Topic management includes a knowledge of what are and are not appropriate topics in particular conversational settings. It also includes an awareness of how speakers change a topic, how they keep a topic going, and how they repair an interaction when a misunderstanding has occurred. Different cultures have different rules and conventions for who can initiate a particular topic and for how they can do it. There are also situation-specific, as well as culture-specific, rules and conventions for who can develop the topic and for how they can do it.

Feedback and Backchannels

An aspect of conversational interaction that is very often not focused on in language learning classrooms is ways of providing feedback, or what are termed *backchannels*—that is, the way in which listeners show they are following what is being said. Speakers might do this verbally, by using such continuers as "mhm," "uh huh," and "yeah"; or by paraphrasing what the other speaker has just said. They might do it nonverbally, by nodding their head, through body position, through degree of closeness, and by maintaining eye contact with the other speaker. They might also "match" a speaker's emotional tone by means of facial expressions, by mirroring the other person's gestures, or by making comments that express sympathy or camaraderie, such as "Oh really?" or "That's awful!" Ways of providing feedback vary cross-culturally, and what may express conversational "alignment" and support in one language may not necessarily have the same effect in another language (Riggenbach 1999).

Repair

Another important conversation strategy that is often not considered in a language classroom is *repair*, that is, the way we correct something that has been said in a conversation. For example, we may correct what we have just said by using *self-repair.*

> *A:* I've just finished reading *Pride and Prejudice* . . . I mean, *War and Peace.*

Or we may correct what has just been said by using *other repair.*

> *A:* I've just finished reading *Pride and Prejudice.* I learned so much about life in Russia.
> *B:* You mean *War and Peace,* don't you?
> *A:* Yeah. That's right. *War and Peace.*

These kinds of conversational convention are as important to teach as are grammar and vocabulary. Focusing on them within the context of conversation as a genre provides both a context of use and a communicative setting that learners are already familiar with, even though they are not always sure of the different sets of rules for participation in their second language.

Approach, Design, and Procedure

A helpful way to summarize the basic principles and procedures in a genre-based language learning program is through the notions of *approach, design,* and *procedure* (Richards and Rodgers 1986). Approach refers to the theory of language and language learning that underlies the particular approach or methodology. Design includes the objectives, organization, and content of the particular syllabus type, kinds of teaching and learning activity, teacher and learner roles, and the role of instructional materials. Procedure describes the actual classroom techniques and practices that might be employed within the particular method or approach.

The view of language that underlies a genre-based language learning classroom is essentially that language is functional; that is, it is through language that we "get things done." Central to this view is the position that language occurs in particular cultural and social contexts and can only be understood in relation to these contexts. Speakers and writers use particular genres to fulfill certain social functions and to achieve certain goals within particular social and cultural contexts. The ways in which language is described may differ between systemic and ESP classrooms, but their underlying view of language as being purposeful and inseparable from the social and cultural context in which it occurs is, as Meriel Bloor (1998) argues, essentially the same.

The theory of language learning that underlies systemic genre work is more explicitly stated than is the theory underlying most ESP discussions of genre-based teaching. Systemic genre-based classrooms draw, in particular, on the notions of scaffolding and *gradual approximation,* that is, the view that learning is best achieved through modeling, guided practice, and then independent construction or performance of new texts. The notion of gradual approximation is also drawn on in ESP classrooms. ESP genre-based course books provide models for students to work with and examples of language learning tasks that could equally be described as examples of scaffolding activities.

The goals and objectives of genre-based language learning programs are to enable learners to use genres that are important for them to be able to participate in and have access to. A genre-based syllabus will be made up of a list of genres learners need to acquire, including relevant discourse and language-level features and contextual information in relation to them. The starting point of the syllabus, however, will be the genre, or whole text, even though lower-level aspects of language will be focused on as well in the course of the program.

Types of teaching and learning activity may be drawn from the wide range of communicative language learning activities currently used in language learning classrooms, including those that focus on understanding language use, accuracy of language use, and fluency in language use. Teachers might also choose to use the teaching and learning cycle that has been described earlier in this chapter. The role of the teacher in a genre-based program is, as with many other contemporary language learning classrooms, one of facilitator and guide for classroom learning. The teacher is also (often) the organizer of instructional materials, although the teacher may, on occasion, ask learners to bring sample texts to the classroom or to observe the performance of a particular genre outside the classroom, which will then form the basis for classroom-based language learning activities. Model texts are, however, particularly important in genre-based classrooms and often provide the initial point of focus in a genre-based language learning lesson. These texts also often provide the basis for joint teacher and student analysis and discussion of the target genre as well as for the joint and independent construction of parallel spoken or written texts.

Teaching techniques and procedures in a genre-based classroom will depend on the aim and general focus of the lesson. Some procedures might focus on certain aspects of language, whereas others might focus on the context of language use. These activities might be sequenced by following the teaching and learning cycle described earlier in this chapter or by starting with *precommunicative activities* (Littlewood 1981), such as form- and accuracy-focused tasks, followed by more communication-oriented activities typical of communicative classrooms. In either case, these tasks should be preceded by a consideration of the context in which the language sample occurs; that is, the best approach is a "top-down" approach that provides the basis for a more "bottom-up" focus on the particular genre and related aspects of language use.

To summarize, whether a genre-based language learning program focuses on spoken and/or written genres depends on students' genre needs and their future contexts of language use. Such programs should include consideration of the relationships between genres and detailed examination of the particular genres students need to control. The following chapters present examples of ways in which aspects of genre knowledge—such as the relationships between genre and context, genre and discourse, and genre and language, as well as appropriacy of content—might be focused on in the language learning classroom.

Tasks and Discussion Questions

1. Genre as an organizing principle for language learning programs

Review Burns and Joyce's (1997) framework for designing a genre-based course, presented in this chapter, and apply their suggested stages to either a language learning situation with which you are familiar or one that you anticipate you might be working in.

2. Systems of genres

Think of a situation where one genre relates to, or presupposes, another genre. For example, what other genres do an academic essay, a job interview, or a letter to the editor presuppose? How do you think these relationships could be accounted for in a language learning program?

3. Event sequences, communication networks, and the language learning classroom

Review the example of an event sequence in this chapter (fig. 1) and draw up an event sequence for a series of genres familiar to you. To get further clarification on your original analysis, interview people who take part in these genres. Use these data to draw up a communication network for the particular system of genres. Choose one of the genres in this communication network, analyze it, and develop classroom tasks following the list of points presented in this chapter in the section on systems of genres and the language learning classroom.

4. Genre and casual conversation

Review the section of this chapter on casual conversations. Ask two native speakers of English for permission to record one of their conversations. Listen to the recording of their conversation and identify as many of the features discussed in this chapter as you can. Then think about how you might use the results of this analysis in a language learning classroom.

5. The teaching and learning cycle

Plan a lesson based around an analysis you have carried out of a particular genre. Base your lesson on the teaching and learning cycle presented in this chapter. Activities you might wish to include in your lesson are

- lead-up activities that focus on the social and cultural context of the text
- lead-up and prediction activities that focus on the content of the text
- lead-up activities that consider

  the purpose of the text
  the speaker or author of the text
  the intended audience of the text
  the setting of the text
  the relationship between participants in the text
  shared understandings between participants in the text
  the tone of the text
  key vocabulary items in the text
  background knowledge assumed by the text
  discourse community expectations
  relationships between the text and other texts

In the lesson you are planning, you might also ask the students

- to identify the discourse structure of the text
- to identify and discuss degrees of formality expressed in the text
- to identify key vocabulary items in the text and group them into categories, such as words that are similar or opposite in meaning or that are in a "whole-part" (e.g., book-chapter, tree-leaves, etc.) relationship with each other
- to make cross-cultural comparisons of conventional aspects of the genre and the social and cultural context of the particular text
- to write a parallel text or to role-play an interaction from the text, working with the analyses they have carried out

If you have an opportunity to teach the lesson, you could afterward reflect on the usefulness of the teaching and learning cycle, making notes under the following headings:

- How successful were you in incorporating the results of your analysis into your lesson?
- How did students respond to the lesson?
- Did students have any problems in the lesson?
- If so, how did you deal with these problems?
- What would you do differently if you taught the lesson again?
- How would you follow up on the lesson?
- How might you adapt the teaching and learning cycle to suit your group of learners or your particular teaching style?

Further Reading

Bazerman, C. 1994. Systems of genres and the enactment of social intentions. In A. Freedman and P. Medway, eds., *Genre and the New Rhetoric.* London: Taylor and Francis.

Bhatia, V. K. 1999. Integrating products, processes, purposes, and participants in professional writing. In C. N. Candlin and K. Hyland, eds., *Writing: Texts, Processes, and Practices.* London: Longman.

Hyon, S. 1996. Genre in three traditions: Implications for ESL. *TESOL Quarterly* 30 (4): 693–722.

Paltridge, B. 1995. An integrated approach to language program development. *English Teaching Forum* 33 (3): 41–44.

Reppen, R. 1995. A genre-based approach to content writing instruction. *TESOL Journal* 4 (2): 32–35.

Richards, J. C., and R. Schmidt. 1983. Conversation analysis. In J. C. Richards and R. Schmidt, eds., *Language and Communication.* London: Longman.

Riggenbach, H. 1999. *Discourse Analysis in the Language Classroom.* Vol. 1, *The Spoken Language.* Ann Arbor: University of Michigan Press. See chapter 1, "Discourse Analysis in the Language Classroom."

Chapter 3

Genre and Context

A genre is clearly much more than just its rhetorical structure and patterns of grammar and vocabulary. Many factors influence a genre, such as the sociocultural context of production and interpretation of the text, the purpose of the text, the audience of the text, expectations of the particular discourse community, and its relationship with other, similar texts. Both the user and the audience of a genre, further, are influenced by their previous experiences with the genre as well as by the content of the text. Thus, teachers need to encourage students to consider the variety of factors, such as reader and writer (or speaker and listener) roles, purpose, and the institutional, social, and cultural values and expectations that influence the production and interpretation of particular texts (Johns 1995a, 1997).

Systemic genre analysts have attempted to deal with this issue by considering the way in which the "context of culture" and "context of situation" of a particular genre impact language choices made within the text. The context of culture includes the attitudes, values, and shared experiences of people living in a particular culture. It also includes culture-specific expectations of ways of behaving and "getting things done," or genres. A context of situation represents situation-specific variables that combine together to produce the particular *register* of a text. These variables include the topic, or content, of the text (its *field*), the relationship between participants in the event (its *tenor*) and the channel of communication (its *mode*). Each of these variables has an impact on the language of a text. For example, field influences such language features as vocabulary choice and verb selection. Tenor influences such aspects of language as expressions of probability, obligation, necessity, attitude, and clause type (such as declarative, interrogative, or imperative). The mode of a text influences, for example, patterns of cohesion and aspects of language that are characteristic of it being a spoken or written text (see chapter 5 for further discussion of the terms *field, tenor,* and *mode* and for a discussion of differences between spoken and written language). The overall generic structure of the text is, in most systemic genre analysts' view, a product of the genre and, in turn, the context of culture—that is, part of a culturally evolved way of doing things—whereas language features are a result of the particular context of situation, or register.

It is clear, then, that not all culturally relevant information can be derived from the text itself. There is also the need to go "beyond the text" into ethnographic examinations of the social and cultural context in which the genre occurs and to explore "insiders' views" on the genre to make genre-based descriptions pedagogically most useful (Tickoo 1994).

An ethnographic view of second language writing considers who writes what to whom, for what purpose, why, when, where, and how; that is, it examines the audience of a text, the writer's purpose, the writing context, and the genre required by the task (Grabe and Kaplan 1996). Ethnographic descriptions of genres can be equally applied to spoken and written texts.

The following examples of the genre "buying a ticket in a tram in Melbourne" show how an ethnographic perspective can be also usefully applied to spoken genres. In this particular interaction, a passenger needs to know, "beyond the text," that he or she can buy a ticket on a tram (as well as at other outlets). Passengers also need to know the various kinds of ticket that are available. For example, a " two-hourly ticket" is one that allows the passenger to travel anywhere on any tram, bus, or train in a particular zone for two hours (including changing trams, buses, or trains in this time period). All of this is part of the shared understandings and assumed background knowledge needed to be able to participate in the particular genre. This is not to say that a person could not travel on a tram without prior knowledge of all of this. However, this knowledge would need to be acquired, in the process of the interaction, for the transaction to be successfully completed.

Example 1

> *Conductor:* Tickets please.
> *Passenger:* Two-hourly.
> *Conductor:* Two dollars ten.
> *Passenger:* Thanks.

Example 2

> *Conductor:* Tickets!
> *Passenger:* Ah . . . four twenty thanks.
> *Conductor:* And eighty cents change.

Example 3

> *Passenger:* Daily concession please.
> *Conductor:* Dollar ten.
> *Passenger:* Does this tram go to Glenferrie Road?
> *Conductor:* No, you'll have to change at Wattletree for a 5.
> *Passenger:* Okay. Thanks.

This is a very situation- and culture-specific interaction. Not all cities in the world, or even in Australia, have trams. Further, tickets cannot always be bought on a tram everywhere in the world, and when they can, it is rare that the ticket will allow a passenger to change between buses, trams, and trains throughout a range of routes for a certain period of time.

A further complication in this particular interaction is that not all trams have a conductor, in which case the ticket has to be bought from the driver or, sometimes, a machine (if they can be bought on the tram at all). The relationship between participants in the genre is also very often fairly informal. Conductors in Melbourne, further, will normally happily give advice on getting about town and other aspects of the city, but a tram driver is usually much less happy to do so. Learners wishing to participate in this genre clearly need more "genre knowledge" than an analysis of the language of the genre alone can provide.

Context-Building Activities

One way to focus classroom activity on aspects of a situation—such as who, what, why, when, and where—is through the use of lead-up tasks that examine the context in which a particular genre occurs. Figure 4 shows how a lesson from a course book can be adapted to include this kind of activity. This example is from Helgesen, Brown, and Smith's *Active Listening: Expanding Understanding through Content, Student's Book 3* (1996) and focuses on casual conversations. Students complete the tasks in pairs or groups as a context-building exercise before listening to

1. Look at the picture.

Who are the people in the picture?
Where are they?
What are they doing?
What do you think they are saying?

2. Listen to the conversation and check your answers.

Fig. 4. A context-building exercise. (Based on Helgesen, Brown, and Smith 1996, 29.)

the text to confirm or correct their predictions. They then continue with further listening tasks based on the conversations in the course book.

Other aspects of genre knowledge, such as appropriate content, can also be dealt with in context-building activities. The example shown in figure 5 is an activity that aims to prepare students to role-play dinner-party conversations. It focuses, in particular, on appropriate and inappropriate conversation topics. Students first ask each other questions to find out about appropriate and inappropriate dinner-party topics in each other's countries. They then interview a number of native speakers of English outside of class and bring this information back to class to discuss and share with each other.

Assumed background knowledge can also be provided by preceding communication tasks with readings that focus on the content students need to be aware of to participate effectively in the genre. For example, part of a lesson on opening a bank account could focus on promotional

At a Dinner Party

1. A Cross-Cultural Comparison: Conversation Topics

What do you usually talk about at a dinner party in your country?
What do you usually not talk about at a dinner party in your country?
Ask and answer these questions with students from other countries, to find out about their countries. Write the students' answers in the chart below:

Name	Country	Usually talked about	Usually not talked about

2. Conversation Topics in the United States

What do people usually talk about at a dinner party in the United States?
What do people usually not talk about at a dinner party in the United States?
Ask an American these questions and complete the chart below:

Usually talked about	Usually not talked about

3. Information Exchange: Conversation Topics

Bring your answers to question 2 to class and compare them with other students' answers.

Fig. 5. Building background knowledge: Conversation topics

material from banks about the various kinds of accounts available. A lesson on finding somewhere to live could include reading material on the various kinds of leasing and rental arrangement in the particular city in which students are living.

Culture notes are another way in which knowledge about appropriate content can be provided to students in the language learning classroom. Deena Levine, Jim Baxter, and Piper McNulty's *The Culture Puzzle: Cross-Cultural Communication for English as a Second Language*

What are polite topics of conversation? What topics are impolite? In some countries, it is impolite to talk about money, politics, or religion. You probably aren't surprised by that. In England, Spain, and other parts of Europe, it is unusual in social situations to talk about work. In the Middle East, people who do business together don't usually talk about their families. In most places, sports, travel, and free-time activities are good things to talk about with someone you don't know very well.

What things do strangers talk about in your country? What topics are impolite?

Fig. 6. A culture note: Conversation topics. (From Helgesen, Brown, and Smith 1996, 34.)

(1987) has many useful examples of culture notes that provide input on important aspects of genre knowledge. Culture notes are also now beginning to appear in a number of more general ESL course books. The example in figure 6 is from an ESL course book that focuses on developing listening skills through content-based instruction.

Another way in which students can be assisted in acquiring an understanding of contextual aspects of genres is through classroom-based context-analysis tasks, such as the one shown in figure 7. The aim of this activity is to help students identify contextual features of texts in a way that helps explain how they are written to match the norms and expectations of a particular audience. This is particularly useful for students who may be reading texts from a different cultural perspective and with different understandings and expectations from those of the writer and intended audience of the text. Resources required for this task are a short written text from one of the students' subject areas and a worksheet like the one shown in figure 7.

Here is a possible procedure to follow for such an activity.

- Choose a short reading text your students would be interested in reading.
- Identify key contextual features of the text, drawing on the categories presented in the worksheet shown in figure 7.
- Prepare prereading comprehension questions that focus on the main point(s) of the text.
- Provide a number of lead-in activities (see "Preparation Activities" in this chapter) to prepare students for reading the text.
- Ask students to read the text to find answers to the comprehension questions.

What is the text about?	
What is the purpose of the text?	
What is the setting of the text (e.g., in a textbook, a newspaper, etc.)?	
What is the tone of the text (e.g., formal, informal, etc.)?	
Who is the author of the text? What is his/her age? sex? ethnic background? social status?	
Who is the intended audience of the text?	
What is the relationship between the author and intended audience of the text?	
What rules or expectations limit how the text might be written?	
What shared cultural knowledge is assumed by the text?	
What shared understandings are implied in the text?	
What other texts does this text assume you have a knowledge of?	
How is the language of the text influenced by each of these factors?	

Fig. 7. A context analysis of a reading text. (Adapted from Paltridge 1999, 167.)

- Ask students to discuss their answers with each other, then have a general feedback session in which the general content of the text is discussed.
- Ask students to reread the text and to use the prepared worksheet to identify key contextual features of the text.
- Ask students to discuss their answers to the questions with each other, then have a general feedback session in which the context and perspective of the text is discussed. Include a discussion of how these contextual aspects impact how the text is both written and read.

- Ask students to write a short description of the context and perspective of the text, based on the notes they have taken in the previous exercise and during the general class discussion.

Students can then be asked to examine texts on other topics or in a different setting (e.g., a newspaper vs. a book) and to discuss how different contextual features may lead to a different style and presentation of the text. It is also helpful for students to discuss how a text in the same genre might be presented in their own language and culture and to identify ways in which the texts might be similar or different from each other. Students can also be asked to discuss how the text they have examined might change if one of the contextual features of the text were changed, such as the author, intended audience, setting, purpose, or subject matter.

Another way in which background knowledge can be built up in the classroom is through lead-in group discussions on the subject matter of the lesson, as well as through the many other lead-in activities teachers typically use in the classroom (see "Preparation Activities" in this chapter). It is important that these sorts of activity precede tasks that assume a particular background knowledge and shared understandings of a particular situation.

Teachers need to teach more than just the genre at hand. They need to teach what students need to "know" to perform a genre, as much as its linguistic and nonlinguistic characteristics. Genres do not exist in a sociocultural vacuum. They are deeply embedded in social and cultural ways of doing things. Every instance of a genre, further, is strongly influenced by the particular context of culture and context of situation in which it occurs. Students need to be as aware of this as they are of the language they need to use to perform particular genres.

Ann Johns (1995a, 1997) gives examples of how students can benefit from carrying out contextual analyses of particular genres. Using several examples of the same genre as catalysts, she invites learners to consider such aspects as

- the discourse community's name or genre category for a particular text
- the values, status, background, education, and needs of readers and writers of a particular genre
- roles and purposes of readers and writers; that is, why someone would write the text and why someone would read it
- typical features of the genre and ways in which these may vary

- similarities that occur among genres and that the students can transfer from one writing situation to another

Johns has done a substantial amount of work with second language learners in the area of genre and audience. This important aspect of the social and cultural context of genres is discussed in the following section.

Genre and Audience

The issue of audience is not widely discussed in much ESL research or taken up in many ESL courses (Johns 1993). This is notwithstanding the fact that for students speaking a second or foreign language, the ability to address a particular audience is essential to their success. As Johns (1993) argues, ESL students "need to develop their understandings of the inter-action between their purposes, the interests and values of real audiences, and the genres that are appropriate for specific rhetorical contexts" (85).

John Swales and Christine Feak (1994) provide an overview of important characteristics of written genres, showing how they are a product of many considerations, such as audience, purpose, organization, style, flow, and presentation. They place audience at the top of their list of considerations.

Spoken genres are equally influenced by the notion of audience. Researchers in the area of conversation analysis, for example, discuss the co-construction of oral interactions, showing how speakers build conversations together on the basis of what the other person has just said and then, with each contribution, create the conditions for what will be said next (Gardner 1995). Attention to audience in these interactions allows speakers to anticipate what might come, where they might make their contribution, and in what way it might be appropriate to do so. This may be through the use of appropriate pairs of utterances, or adjacency pairs; through the use of preferred and dispreferred responses; through the use of particular turn-taking strategies; and by providing other speakers with appropriate feedback and backchannels to show attention to what is being said.

The notion of audience is encoded in grammar as we speak. We do not chat just to "kill time" but rather to clarify and to extend the interpersonal relations that have brought us together. The way in which language is used in spoken interactions is influenced by the relationship between the speakers, the frequency with which they come into contact, the degree of affective involvement they have with each other, and their sense of affiliation for each other (Eggins and Slade 1997). The ways in which these factors influence language include choices in vocabulary, the use of direct or indirect speech acts, mood choices (e.g., whether we use a declarative, imperative, or interrogative form), and choice of modal items that express degrees of polarity ("yes" or "no"), probability, certainty, usuality, and obligation. For example, the use of such items as "definitely," "probably," "might," "perhaps," and "should" is influenced as much by audience as by what is being talked about.

A focus on audience is especially important in second language writing classrooms. Indeed, the very first task in Swales and Feak's (1994) *Academic Writing for Graduate Students: Essential Tasks and Skills* focuses on the issue of audience. They give examples of the same sentence written in two different ways, for two different audiences, and ask students to consider in what way they are different and why. Students then write one-sentence definitions of a term in their own particular field for two different audiences: one for a graduate student in a totally unrelated field and one for a fellow student in their own area. They then exchange definitions and discuss how the definitions differ.

The distinction between "general" and "particular" expectations of discourse communities, or audiences, is especially helpful for students who are learning to write in academic settings (Dudley-Evans 1995a). *General expectations,* refers to general transferable patterns of textual organization that might be transferred from one area of study to another, such as the overall organization of a thesis or a journal article. *Particular expectations* refers to the ways in which the general patterns need to be adapted to meet the expectations and requirements of particular fields of study. General expectations can be taught in general classes, whereas particular expectations can best be explored in discipline, or subject-specific, groups or in one-to-one tutorials. Developing this kind of discipline-specific sensitivity should, in Dudley-Evans's view, form part of the teaching of academic writing. An approach to the teaching of academic writing that implies that there are common patterns of organization that always apply in all disciplines can be dangerously misleading (Dudley-Evans 1993).

Arthur Brookes and Peter Grundy, in their book *Writing for Study Purposes: A Teacher's Guide to Developing Individual Writing Skills* (1990), provide a number of consciousness-raising activities that focus on the relationship between readers and writers of texts. In the exercise shown in figure 8, students consider the primary and secondary readership of

1. Divide a page into three vertical columns with these headings:

   Writing Activity   *Primary Readership*   *Secondary Readership*

   In the first column, list types of writing that you do, then fill in the primary and secondary readerships. Example:

Writing Activity	*Primary Readership*	*Secondary Readership*
postcard sent from holiday	friend who receives it	other people who may pick it up
official letter	addressee	colleagues reading file

2. Divide another sheet of paper into four columns with these headings:

Primary Reader Group	*Genre*	*Writer*	*Secondary Reader Group*

   Under the four headings, list the groups you belong to as a primary reader, the genre this readership relates to, the writer/s of these genres, and any individuals or groups who are secondary readers. Example:

Primary Reader Group	*Genre*	*Writer*	*Secondary Reader Group*
committee members	minutes	secretary	management
students	textbooks	authors	publishers/critics/ teachers

Fig. 8. Writing and readers: Some consciousness-raising activities. (Adapted from Brookes and Grundy 1990, 19.)

their texts. As Brookes and Grundy point out, the notion of secondary readership is often neglected in the second language writing literature, even though it is often of considerable importance.

Brookes and Grundy also provide a number of other activities in readership awareness. In one of their suggested exercises, students do a detailed analysis of their "personality type" and pass it on to another student, who writes a short text about the other student taking these factors into account. They also suggest an exercise for the kind of writing in which the specific reader is much less clearly known, such as in a university assignment, thesis, or job application. In this exercise, students may focus on a job that a member of the class might reasonably apply for in an English–speaking country. One group of students lists the qualities and experience needed for the job; another group lists the job-specific achievements, qualities, and interests of particular students in the class. The students then come together and decide how they can best set out the qualities and achievements of the "job applicant" with the expectations of the employer. A writing preparation exercise like this can be equally employed in preparing students for spoken genres, such as job interviews. The notes students take can be used to prepare for sets of expected interview questions, then students can draw on their notes in role-play activities that focus on the particular genre.

A further exercise asks students to order material from a reader's perspective. For example, students choose a city and, in groups, write one-paragraph explanations of why a person would enjoy living in that city, with each student group choosing a different audience for its paragraph (e.g., an old person, a young person, a parent, a businessman). Students could do similar tasks in preparation for giving oral presentations on their favorite city, as they role-play showing someone around their hometown, or as preparation for the dinner-party conversation topic "Where do you come from?"

Tricia Hedge, in her book *Writing* (1988), discusses the issue of audience in a section titled "Who Am I Writing For?" In her view, it is much more motivating for students if the pieces of writing they do in class can become genuine pieces of communication with real audiences, such as other students, visitors, the local newspaper, or organizations. Suggestions she gives for these kinds of text include letters of invitation and thanks to guest speakers, letters to the editor, and information leaflets for newcomers to the language center in which the students are studying. She also points out that teachers can enter into writer–reader relationships with their students by responding to students' texts rather than simply assessing them. Spoken genres, such as introducing a guest speaker, thank-you speeches, and showing new students around the language center, can be prepared for in a similar way.

Christopher Tribble (1996) provides suggestions for activities that give learners the opportunity to prepare for communicating with real audiences. One activity he describes draws together student expertise and content knowledge and the production of audience-oriented texts (Tribble 1996, 147–48). In this activity, each student chooses something he or she can do and would like to explain to another member of the class. Each student finds another student in the class who would like to be able to perform the same task and finds out how much that student already knows about the task. Each student then writes a text explaining the activity to their student partner, taking account of what the partner both knows and does not know about the task. The partner then reads and assesses the text to see if it provides sufficient information and is sufficiently clear for him or her to be able to understand, and perhaps carry out, the particular activity. If it is not, the reader returns the text to the writer, who then revises it in light of the reader's feedback on the text. Students could equally prepare spoken presentations with the same purpose and have other students evaluate and provide feedback in a similar way. This kind of task is particularly useful for helping students focus on what their audience already knows about a topic and on targeting their (spoken or written) text to a specific audience.

Language clearly is not enough. Students need an understanding of the sociocultural context and setting of a genre, as well as the relationship between themselves and the audience(s) of their texts. They need to understand the purpose of each text and what context, setting, audience, and purpose imply for a text's "positioning," style, content, and form. Students need to be aware of shared understandings between participants, discourse community expectations, and the background knowledge that participants assume of each other in their performance of a particular genre. Students also need to know what they can appropriately write or talk about in the particular genre. Knowledge of generic structures, grammar, and vocabulary are necessary but are clearly not sufficient to effectively participate in a genre.

One way in which aspects of genre knowledge can be focused on in the language learning classroom is through the use of appropriately focused preparation activities. The following section provides suggestions for these kinds of activity.

Preparation Activities

The aim of preparation activities is to help learners understand the genre they are focusing on, the audience for the particular genre, and the context in which the genre occurs. These activities should also aim to activate learners' background knowledge in relation to the particular genre; that is, the activities should aim to find out what the learners already know about the genre, the context in which it occurs, and language features associated with it, rather than assuming that learners have no previous experience of the particular genre. Preparation activities should also aim to familiarize learners with the topic (in general) of the text under focus. They should, however, avoid providing the complete content of the text; that is, they should avoid leaving "no new information" for students to uncover about the genre being studied. Preparation activities should also raise learners' interest, create expectations, and "set the scene" for the tasks that follow them.

Examples of preparation activities include previewing activities, vocabulary development activities, and activities using lead-in questions. In previewing activities, students might preview

the social and cultural context of the genre	from	the title or topic of the text
the content of the text		visuals
the genre		key words
key vocabulary items		discussion questions or focus questions, concerning, for example, who, where, what, and why

Vocabulary development activities include

brainstorming related vocabulary
predicting vocabulary and putting related words into groups
eliciting/preteaching key (rather than least known) vocabulary items
matching key vocabulary items to pictures

Activities using lead-in questions might employ questions related to

the social and cultural context of the text
the setting of the text
the content of the text
the genre
the speaker or author of the text
the audience of the text
the relationship between participants in the genre
the purpose of the genre
the tone of the genre
key vocabulary items
assumed background knowledge of the text

Depending on the level of the learner group, lead-in questions might take the form of multiple-choice questions, true/false questions, gap-filling tasks, or more open discussion questions.

Learners might then be given comprehension questions aimed at providing them with an overall understanding of the text. They might also be asked to listen to or read the text to confirm or correct their expectations or to extract specific information from the text. Students might then relisten or reread for detailed comprehension and to work out meanings of further key vocabulary items from the context of the text. Students can also be asked to compare and discuss the instance of the genre they are examining with an example of the same genre in their own language and culture.

When choosing a particular genre to focus on, it is important to remember that the sample text(s) should be relevant to the learners' immediate and longer-term interests and needs. The aim of the activities should be to help learners understand the text, rather than to test their comprehension. The activities should be designed so that learners do not simply have to get a "right answer" but have to listen or read to carry the activities out.

Preparation activities should aim to develop the strategies that competent speakers and writers of a language use when meeting a new text (e.g., predicting; confirming and/or correcting predictions). They should aim to develop a range of strategies that are appropriate to the texts they are designed for, be transferable to other texts and tasks, and be designed so that learners can use them independently outside the classroom. Preparation activities should also aim to encourage learners to draw on prior knowledge and experience in their first language and culture and on what they already know, and can do, in English.

Students Doing Their Own Genre Analysis

Such writers as Ann Johns (1997), John Swales (1990), and Paul Prior (1995) argue strongly for having students carry out ethnographic investigations of the genres they need to acquire and the contexts in which these genres occur. As these writers argue, teachers can help students "become ethnographers." For example, teachers can ask students to consider the roles that they and their instructors play in their classes, the main topics and concepts covered in their classes, and how each of these interrelate with each other. Students can also be asked to examine the specific writing or speaking conventions and expectations in particular areas of language use, the purpose of the pieces of genre they may be required to produce, and the kinds of knowledge claim that are permissible in their particular field of study or employment.

Points that need to be considered in these investigations include the social and cultural context of a genre, the content of the genre, and the role of the speaker or author of the genre. It is also important to consider the intended audience of the genre and the relationship between participants in the genre. Other important aspects that need to be considered include the purpose, setting, and tone of the genre and typical discourse-level and grammatical features of the genre. Discourse community expectations, shared understandings, and assumed background knowledge also need to be explored, as do the relationships between the genre being studied and other genres. Students can do this by using ethnographic techniques, such as interviews, observations, and "field notes," combined with their own detailed analyses of sample texts. The results of these investigations can be brought to class and used as the basis for discussion and the production of students' own texts. Teachers need to train students to observe and describe how and why language is used in particular ways in the genres the students need to be able to use.

Sally Burgess (1997) holds a similar view, advocating an approach in which students engage in genre analysis as equal partners with their instructors to arrive at a heightened awareness of discourse norms and the social purposes these norms fulfill. In her view, such an approach has a greater potential to provide students with the mastery of genre conventions than does engaging in teacher-constructed tasks alone.

Ann Johns (1990) also discusses the use of learning logs that students write as part of the process of discovering rules of use in communicative settings that are foreign to them. An advantage of these logs is that they allow for individual dialogue between the teacher and the student yet remain private to both parties. They also have the added advantage of promoting fluency in writing and a forum for analysis of the particular context of use.

The focus of these writers is thus on student discovery and, in particular, what Ann Johns, in her book *Text, Role, and Context: Developing Academic Literacies* (1997), terms "students as researchers." As Johns argues, while teachers cannot hope to predict all of their students' possible future genre use, teachers can help students "to ask questions of texts, of contexts—and of themselves" (92) to help them produce and interpret the kinds of text they need to command.

Tasks and Discussion Questions

1. Sociocontextual aspects of genres

Select several examples of a genre that would be useful for a particular group of students to examine in class. Consider what students need to know "beyond the text" to understand this text. How might you go about bringing this to their attention?

2. Genre and context

Do a context analysis of a spoken or written genre based on the framework presented in figure 7 in this chapter. Suggest how you could use the results of this analysis in your classroom.

3. Content and genre knowledge

Read chapter 1 of Carol Berkenkotter and Thomas Huckin's book *Genre Knowledge in Disciplinary Communication: Cognition/Culture/Power* (1995)—or Ulla Connor's summary of their chapter in her book *Contrastive Rhetoric: Cross-Cultural Aspects of Second Language Writing* (1996, 128–29)—and summarize what they have to say about genre, content, and background knowledge. Then choose a language learning course book and look at how content (other than linguistic content) and background knowledge is dealt with in the text. For example, if the book focuses on teaching writing business letters or on social interactions, what does the course book have to say about appropriate content. What could you add to the teaching material that would be useful for a group of learners?

4. Genre and audience

Read Ann Johns's article "Genre and Pedagogical Purposes" (1995a) and do a similar audience analysis of a particular spoken or written genre. Suggest ways you could use the results of this analysis in a language learning classroom (including getting students to do a similar analysis of their own).

5. Genre and background knowledge

Choose a spoken or written genre that requires a substantial amount of background knowledge to understand it, or to carry it out, effectively. Collect some authentic examples of the genre, and consider what students need to know "beyond the text" of the examples to understand the genre or to carry it out.

Further Reading

Berkenkotter, C., and T. N. Huckin. 1995. *Genre Knowledge in Disciplinary Communication: Cognition/Culture/Power.* Hillsdale, NJ: Lawrence Erlbaum. See chapter 1, "Rethinking Genre from a Sociocognitive Perspective."

Connor, U. 1996. *Contrastive Rhetoric: Cross-Cultural Aspects of Second Language Writing.* Cambridge: Cambridge University Press. See pp. 126–29, "The Concept of Genre."

Grabe, W., and R. Kaplan. 1996. *Theory and Practice of Writing: An Applied Linguistic Perspective.* London: Longman. See chapter 4, pp. 106–11, "Postsecondary Writing and Discourse Communities."

Johns, A. M. 1995. Genre and pedagogical purposes. *Journal of Second Language Writing* 4 (2): 181–90.

Johns, A. M. 1997. *Text, Role, and Context: Developing Academic Literacies.* Cambridge: Cambridge University Press. See chapter 4, "Discourse Communities and Communities of Practice"; chapter 6, "Students as Researchers."

Swales, J. M. 1990. *Genre Analysis. English in Academic and Research Settings.* Cambridge: Cambridge University Press. See chapter 2, "The Concept of Discourse Community."

Tribble, C. 1996. *Writing.* Oxford: Oxford University Press. See chapter 6, "Approaches to the Teaching of Writing: Genre."

Chapter 4
Genre and Discourse

Several different terms have been used in the literature on genre analysis to describe the discourse structure of written and spoken genres. In ESP genre work, the discourse structure of texts is often described as being made up of *moves,* which are labeled according to authorial purpose and the conventions of the particular discourse community. Moves may occur in a cycling pattern; that is, combinations of moves may repeat themselves within the text.

The term *generic structure* is used in Australian genre work to refer to genre-specific discourse structures, such as the discourse structure of a lecture, service encounter, business letter, academic essay, or recipe. This term is often used interchangeably with the term *schematic structure.*

The term *text type* describes patterns of discourse organization that occur across different genres, such as description, narrative, instruction, explanation, definition, exemplification, classification, compare-and-contrast, cause-and-effect, discussion, argument, and problem-solution texts. In some of the Australian genre literature, some of these text types are called genres.

Suggestions for focusing on discourse-level aspects of genres appear in books and articles on genre analysis and in teacher-oriented books on discourse analysis. Some of these suggestions are summarized in this chapter. Some of the suggested activities apply only to spoken genres, others apply only to written genres, and some may be applied to both spoken and written genres.

Focusing on Written Genres

Writing arguments. Ken Hyland (1990) provides an extremely useful analysis of the argumentative academic essay (see fig. 9). He breaks his analysis up into the text's main stages, each of which contains a number

Stage	Move
1. Thesis	(Gambit) a controversial or dramatic statement (Information) presents background information on the topic of the essay Proposition states the writer's position and delimits the topic (Evaluation) brief support for the proposition (Marker) signposts the direction of the essay
2. Argument	Marker signals the claim and relates it to the text (Restatement) rephrasing or repetition of the proposition Claim reason for acceptance of the proposition. Either a. strength of perceived shared assumptions, or b. generalization based on data or evidence, or c. force of conviction Support states grounds that underpin the claim. Either by a. explicating assumptions used to make the claim, or b. providing data or references
3. Conclusion	(Marker) signals conclusion boundary Consolidation relates argument to the proposition (Affirmation) restates proposition (Close) widens context or perspective of proposition

Fig. 9. The structure of the argumentative essay. (From Hyland 1990, 69.)

of moves. The elements in parentheses in his analysis represent optional components in the text; that is, the move need not occur but will appear in that position if it does.

The framework for the discourse structure of an argument shown in figure 10 provides a further model for students to draw on to write their own argument texts—in this case, within the context of a letter to the editor. The presentation of this model is preceded by a discussion of the social and cultural contexts in which arguments occur, an examination of the aim and purpose of arguments, and an analysis and discussion of sample texts. Students then use the framework for drafting a letter to the editor. The writing also includes comparison of student texts, peer revision, and editing. The final texts are put together as a class news sheet of letters to the editor on the topic under discussion.

Other authors have also made suggestions for the teaching of discourse patterns in written genres. John Swales and Christine Feak's

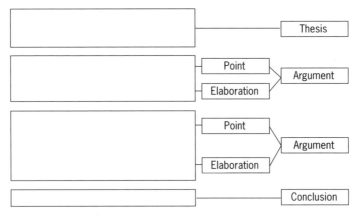

Fig. 10. A framework for writing an argument. (From Knapp and Watkins 1994, 131.)

Academic Writing for Graduate Students: Essential Tasks and Skills (1994), Robert Weissberg and Suzanne Buker's *Writing Up Research: Experimental Report Writing for Students of English* (1990), and Tony Dudley-Evans's *Writing Laboratory Reports* (1985) provide many examples of the application of the results of genre analysis in the teaching of written genres in the language learning classroom.

John Swales's work has always included many helpful suggestions for focusing on discourse-level aspects of written genres in the language learning classroom. These include using color-coded texts, reassembly exercises, comparing student texts, writing from research cards, data commentaries, and rhetorical consciousness raising.

Using color-coded texts. In this exercise, students are presented with texts that have been "marked up" and color-coded to indicate their generic or "text" structure. These color-coded texts are used both for developing discourse appreciation through reading and as a preparation for writing. Robert Weissberg and Suzanne Buker (1990, 91–92) provide an example of an already analyzed "marked-up" text (the methods section of a research report) that is presented to students for discussion purposes. John Swales and Christine Feak (1994) also provide examples of "marking-up exercises" in which students are given discourse categories, such as "situation-problem-solution," and asked to locate the relevant sections in a sample text.

Reassembly exercises. Reassembly exercises involve cutting up texts into stages, or moves, and jumbling them for reassembly. This can be carried out with individual sentences as well. Tony Dudley-Evans (1995b) provides an example of a reordering exercise in which students are given jumbled sentences from a text and asked to put them in the correct order. After students have done this, the correct order is discussed, and the overall move structure of the genre is introduced and explained. The discussion is followed by detailed practice of the language used to express each of the particular moves.

Comparing student texts. Students can be asked to compare texts written by members of the class for the same purpose. The comparison can be based on some set of guidelines, such as a list of key aspects of language and content covered earlier in the course. In this exercise, students use the list of points to critique each other's texts. They then discuss their observations on each text with the student who wrote it. Each student then reworks his or her text on the basis of these observations. In this approach, students work with "apprentice" exemplars (Flowerdew 2000) rather than "expert" models, as a way of motivating students to work on and improve their own pieces of writing.

Writing from research cards. Writing from research cards involves the writing of texts based on simulated library research cards plus the title and an abstract, or summary, of the text. An example of this kind of task can be found in *Writing Up Research* (Weissberg and Buker 1990, 60–62), where students are asked to write a literature review from a provided outline. Tony Dudley-Evans (1995b) describes a similar exercise in which students write a text based on some data or information provided. To write up the data or information in an appropriate manner, they have to draw on what has been taught in the rest of the course and on their own experience. Dudley-Evans found these exercises very successful in helping students bring together and consolidate both what they have learned from the course materials and their overall knowledge of the particular genre on which they were focusing.

Data commentaries. John Swales and Christine Feak (1994) provide examples of data commentary activities in which they guide students beyond the transformation of information toward the more challenging task of writing a commentary on nonverbal data. In their view, activities focused on information transfer often operate against critical thinking, reading, and writing. They suggest that a switch from information transfer to data commentary can be more useful for helping students learn this important aspect of academic reading and writing.

Rhetorical consciousness raising. In using genre-based tasks in the classroom, the "problem of content" may loom large; that is, teachers may find it difficult to present students with appropriate and relevant content when students in the same class have different interests and different subject specializations (Swales 1990). One suggestion Swales (1995) provides for dealing with this is to have students carry out small-scale surveys of the rhetorical and linguistic practices in their own fields of study. Students then compare the results of their analysis with other students' analyses and note the similarities and differences. Swales describes these rhetorical consciousness-raising activities as one way of dealing with discipline-specific variation in the genres students are learning to write.

Ann Johns (1993) gives a further example of this kind of task. She suggests providing students with a task in which the audience of their text is clearly known and getting them to gather data about the audience that they can then use in deciding how to present their particular argument. She gives an example in which students wrote to university trustees and state legislators regarding a proposed increase in fees at the university at which the students were studying. To carry out this task, the students considered their readers' prior knowledge and particular interests and the particular approach to argumentation that would appeal to them. The students collected such information as annual reports, past public statements, and information from the university's administrators about particular trustees' views. They also made phone calls to legislators' local offices and interviewed their assistants, asking for such information as their political views and their views on education.

Having gathered this information, her students asked themselves several questions: What do the readers value? What values are most important to them, and what values are least important to them? What is my purpose in writing to this particular person? How can I revise my claim on the basis of what I now know about my audience? The students then commenced drafting their letters, referring back to these questions as they revised their texts. The "intended audience," its values, and its interests were thus a crucial factor in the shaping of the students' texts.

Students can be trained to "act as researchers" as a way of helping them write texts that meet the institutional and audience expectations of their particular field and discover the knowledge and skills that are necessary for membership in their particular academic community (Johns 1997). This might involve identifying key topics and concepts in their particular area, as well as exploring the writing conventions of their particular field of study and the kinds of knowledge claim that are permissible in the particular area.

Other examples of studies that examine discourse community expectations can be found in Diane Belcher and George Braine's *Academic Writing in a Second Language: Essays in Research and Pedagogy* (1995). For example, Ann Johns's "Teaching Classroom and Authentic Genres: Initiating Students into Academic Cultures and Discourses," Paul Prior's "Redefining the Task: An Ethnographic Examination of Writing and Response in Graduate Seminars," and Christine Casanave's "Local Interactions: Constructing Contexts for Composing in a Graduate Sociology Program" each take up this topic in slightly different ways. They each highlight, however, the importance of taking a contextualized view of student writing and avoiding simplistic views of discourse communities as being somehow monolithic and unchanging.

Rhetorical consciousness-raising activities, then, are exploratory in nature (Sengupta 1999). They may include a focus on linguistic and rhetorical strategies as well as a focus on shared knowledge and values and how these impact what is said and how it is said. This kind of knowledge provides students with access to genres that, hopefully, will enable them to participate more successfully in particular communicative settings. Louise Delpit (1998) argues strongly for teaching these aspects of genres, saying that if you are not already a part of the culture of power, "being explicitly told the rules of that culture makes acquiring power easier" (282). In contrast, Alan Luke (1996) argues that learning dominant genres leads to uncritical reproduction of the status quo and does not necessarily provide the kind of access that teachers hope their teaching might provide for learners. Others, such as Frances Christie (1989), argue that empowering learners through making explicit the way in which writers make their meanings gives learners access to the "hidden curriculum" of education and power. Patricia Bizzell (1992) presents a similar view, saying that teachers need to help students master the language and culture of the curriculum. The key question, however, is how can teachers do this?

Other writers, such as Ruth Spack (1998), have pointed out that what academic writing is and what ESL students need to know to produce it is not a simple matter. Spack points to Bizzell's (1982) suggestion for a sociocontextual approach to examining academic knowledge, an approach that emphasizes the relationship between discourse, community, and knowledge. As Spack points out, teachers need to do more than just examine the finished product. Teachers also need to examine the process through which writers produce texts, including an understanding of the particular sets of values that underlie them. This takes learners beyond conventions and generic forms to an understanding of the contexts in which these conventions and forms occur (Zamel 1998). As Tony Silva and his colleagues have pointed out, students often ask for model texts, but teachers are sometimes reluctant to provide them, fearing they will lead to imitation rather than creativity and learning (Silva, Reichelt, and Lax-Farr 1994). The challenge for the teacher is how to draw these two tensions together, that is, how to provide learners with guidance and direction yet at the same time foster independence and learning.

Students doing their own "on-line" genre analysis. John Flowerdew (1993) discusses activities in which students do their own "on-line" genre analysis. In these activities, students create a text by examining other examples of a particular genre and replicating their features. For example, students can be given business letters to examine. They work out how this kind of text is typically written, then write texts of their own based on the model texts they have examined. Flowerdew argues strongly for the use of such parallel texts in language learning classrooms, saying that they inevitably reveal patterns of discourse, grammar, and vocabulary that are not available in dictionaries, grammar books, or, indeed, many course books.

Translation based on a sample of instances of a given genre. Genre-based activities can also involve translation from the students' first language into English (Flowerdew 1993). Students start with a sample of instances of a particular genre in their first language and then write a similar text in their second language. As they do this, they should consider similarities and differences in such areas as discourse structure, vocabulary and verb choice, and the use of formulaic expressions and honorifics. This activity is different, Flowerdew points out, from tasks of grammar translation, which typically focus more on sentence-level issues than on the discourse-level and contextual aspects of texts.

Christopher Tribble (1996), in his book on writing for language teachers, also provides discourse-oriented tasks that are useful for genre-based language learning classrooms. These include an exercise that focuses on analyzing and presenting aspects of textual organization.

Analyzing and presenting aspects of textual organization. In this task, students are given a text on a topic of interest to them; the text is cut up into discourse segments and jumbled. In groups, students agree on a sequence for the text, giving each section of the text a functional label (e.g., "situation," "problem," "solution"; "general," "particular"). They then prepare a class presentation in which they explain their reasons for their sequencing of the text, using the labels they chose to describe their text. This type of task particularly helps students develop an awareness of both the linguistic and extralinguistic information readers draw on to establish a text's coherence.

Vijay Bhatia, in his book *Analysing Genre: Language Use in Profes-*

sional Settings (1993), also provides suggestions for teaching discourse-level aspects of genres. These include identifying and assigning discourse values to parts of a text and introducing learners to variation in specific moves.

Identifying and assigning discourse values to parts of a text. This activity involves the teacher "marking up" the discourse structure of a text and preparing an accompanying worksheet that explains the functional labels given to each of the moves in the text. Students use this explanation to identify the same moves in another text. A model answer is then provided for the students to check their answers against. An advantage of this kind of task is that it can be used both in class and in a self-access situation, as the materials are both explanatory and task-directed.

Introducing learners to variation in specific moves. This activity follows the same pattern as the previous activity except that it focuses on variation in the realization of moves. Students are provided with an explanation of a particular discourse strategy (e.g., the way in which a businessperson might thank customers for their support). Students then look at examples of the genre to see how authors have gone about expressing the move. They consider reasons for differences between different authors' realization of moves. An answer key is again provided.

Comparing and contrasting categories of genre and text type. Students can be presented with a number of categories of genre and text type and asked to select the appropriate categories for particular texts. For example, they could look at examples of letters to the editor, book reviews, or essays and identify which are, for example, instances of description, argument, explanation, or cause-and-effect texts—or a combination of these. A useful point that comes out of this activity is that one genre (e.g., letters to the editor or essays) may present examples of a range of different text types. It is also useful to point out that the text type of an essay, for example, is often a result of a particular essay question that contains a key word (e.g., *describe, discuss,* or *explain*) to indicate the particular essay type desired.

Identifying generic structure and text structure components. Students may also be given a list of generic and text structure components and asked to locate them within a particular text. For example, they might identify an essay's title, introduction, body, conclusion, and references; then whether the essay is, for example, a problem-solution, compare-and-contrast, or exposition text; and finally the relevant text structure components.

Reconstructing a text from structural and content information. For this activity, students are presented with the generic and text structure of a text and asked to reconstruct it from this information plus a list of key content words and other supporting information. For example, students can be given the generic and text structure of a letter of complaint plus relevant background information and can then be asked to write a letter in response to a particular situation (see Hammond et al. 1992 for material that can be used for this activity; see Paltridge 1996 for an analysis of the generic structure and text structure of a letter of complaint).

Matching generic and text structure components to sections of a text. This task involves the teacher marking up a sample text into its generic and text structure components and then cutting the text up into each of the sections identified in the analysis. Students are then given slips of paper on which are written the generic and text structure components of the particular text and are asked to match these structural components to the relevant section(s) of the text. They then arrange the jumbled sections of the text into its original sequence.

Identifying similarities and differences in terms of generic structures and accompanying text types. Students may also be asked to analyze genres—such as lectures, seminar presentations, and essays—for similarities and differences in terms of generic structures and accompanying text types. They can then be asked to create texts of their own, drawing on the language and discourse patterns identified in the texts they have already examined. This kind of task is useful in helping students identify discourse patterns (e.g., problem-solution and general-particular) that can be generalized across genres. It is also useful for helping students see that whereas some genres may have a typical generic structure, there are other genres (e.g., lectures) for which this is often much less the case.

The text shown in figure 11 was written by a student who carried out this kind of task. The analysis of its discourse structures shows the typical generic structure of an academic essay and text structures typical of problem-solution and description texts. In the activities that preceded the writing of this text, the student listened to a lecture, did guided reading, and gave a seminar presentation. Each of these activities focused on the different genres as instances of problem-solution texts. Students completing these activities had been exposed to several models of this kind of rhetorical structure before they wrote their own texts. Students were also familiar with descriptions, from other discourse-focused activities they had done in the course.

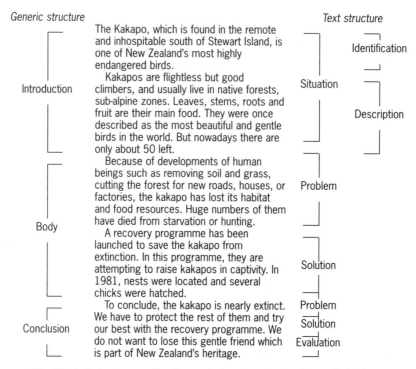

Fig. 11. A student essay: Problem-solution/description. (From Paltridge 1995a, 509.)

Analyzing assignment and examination questions to identify the appropriate text types. Students may also be asked to analyze assignment and examination questions to identify the appropriate text type for each particular question. They can then draw up for each particular assignment or examination question what Michael McCarthy and Ronald Carter (1994) term a *text frame*, that is, a diagrammatic representation of the structural organization of their answer to the question, which students can use to write their own individual texts.

Other Activities

Other activities that aim to build an awareness of how written genres are organized at the discourse level include

- giving students sections of a text cut up into stages and jumbled for the students to reassemble
- giving students sentences taken from a section of a text, cut up, and jumbled for the students to reassemble

- asking students to match headings to sections of a text
- giving students jumbled summaries to sequence while or after reading a text
- asking students to look at a written text and note how it begins and ends
- giving students the typescript of an authentic written text and asking them to mark the stages in the text
- giving students a skeleton of a text (e.g., functional labels for the stages of the text, key vocabulary items, discourse markers, opening and closing sections of the texts and some of the key sections in between) and asking them to complete the text

Focusing on Spoken Genres

The notion of genre as a "purposeful, socially-constructed, communicative event" (Nunan 1991, 44) is especially useful for teaching spoken language. Different genres have their own distinctive discourse, or generic, structures, which can be usefully focused on in a language learning classroom (Nunan 1991). Nunan proposes a "top-down" approach to teaching spoken genres, starting with larger elements (e.g., contextual aspects and discourse features) and concluding with smaller ones (e.g., grammar and vocabulary). Nunan takes this argument up further in his book *Second Language Teaching and Learning* (1999), where he reiterates the importance of making whole texts the point of departure in course design, placing genre at the center of his argument. Tricia Hedge, in *Teaching and Learning in the Language Classroom* (2000), also highlights the value of genre for the teaching of spoken language, showing how the notion of genre enables us to identify different types of speaking situation and their characteristics for teaching and learning purposes.

Spoken genres that have been studied in the area of academic English include lectures, the graduate seminar, plenary lectures and poster session discussions at academic conferences, and college laboratory sessions. John Flowerdew (1994a) provides a helpful overview of the research relevant to second language lecture comprehension. As he observes, relatively little work has been done toward analyzing the discourse structure of lectures compared with other genres, such as the research article, and what has been done raises more questions than it answers. In his view, a lot more research is needed before we have a clear idea of what constitutes a successful second language lecture.

Susan Thompson (1994) carried out an analysis of eighteen lecture introductions from a range of disciplines. She found it difficult, however, to identify a straightforward pedagogic model for academic lectures. She also reports problems in identifying a typical order of units. She concluded that there is no typical structure of lecture introductions but rather a largely unpredictable mix of a small set of what she calls *functions* (e.g., setting up the lecture framework) and *subfunctions* (e.g., indicating the scope of the lecture).

John Flowerdew and Lindsay Miller (1996) describe a helpful investigation into second language lectures that goes beyond the textual dimension of the genre. They found a discrepancy in student and lecturer perceptions in terms of the purposes of lectures, the roles of lecturers, styles of lecturing, the use of simplified language in lectures, listener behavior, and the use of humor in lectures. As they argue, preparation for lectures in a second language should not be concerned simply with the decoding of language features. They recommend conducting presessional training courses for lecturers and students with the goal of preparing second language students for what they call the "whole new culture of learning."

A study that examined graduate seminars in the United States found them to be a rather "hybrid" speech event that appeared to comprise four "subgenres" (Weissberg 1993). These subgenres were proposals, in-progress reports, preliminary literature reviews, and completed research reports, each with their own (although in some ways similar) rhetorical structures. Weissberg also found a noticeable gap between professors' expectations and nonnative students' actual seminar presentations. The professors he interviewed said they preferred more "audience-friendly" oral presentations, whereas many of the students that were observed gave what were instead oral versions of written genres.

Conversation management tasks. Guy Cook (1989), in his book on discourse analysis for language teachers, provides a conversation management task that is useful for second language learners, especially as an awareness-raising activity or a "discussion starter" on the subject of conversation management in different languages and cultures. His task is shown in figure 12. The task is clearly written from the perspective of someone teaching English in Britain. It can, however, be easily adapted to other teaching situations, such as teaching English in the United States or abroad.

Using culture notes. One way in which students can be provided with information about discourse-level aspects of spoken genres is through the use of culture notes. *The Culture Puzzle: Cross-Cultural*

In Russian culture, the following appear to be more frequent features of interaction than they are in British culture:

— the absence of a translation equivalent of "goodbye" at the end of a telephone call
— long uninterrupted turns during casual conversation
— the use of the sound conventionally written in English "uh huh" or "mhuh" in English, with a voice quality which in English can indicate boredom
— interruption of a speaker to say that what he or she is saying is already known to the hearer
— asking directly, and without elaborate apology, for small favors: for example, a cigarette, a coin for the telephone, etc.
— comment by older people upon the behavior and dress of younger people
— standing up for elderly people on public transport
— offering food to visitors

1. Which of these, if any, do you think someone teaching Russian students English should attempt to make them change when they are speaking English?
2. Make a list of similar differences between British culture and one you are familiar with and consider how you would approach them when teaching English.

Fig. 12. Conversation management: A cross-cultural comparison. (From Cook 1989, 124.)

Communication for English as a Second Language (Levine, Baxter, and McNulty 1987) provides many examples of the use of this approach to providing students with information about aspects of conversations that vary across cultures. The example shown in figure 13 focuses on ways of saying goodbye and, in particular, on the fact that such expressions as "I'll see you later" are not meant to be taken literally. In *The Culture Example,* this text is followed by language practice activities that focus on this aspect of conversation interactions.

The example of a culture note in figure 14 is from a recent ESL listening textbook's unit on conversational interactions. In the textbook, the culture note is preceded and followed by listening and discussion tasks. The text then provides a speaking activity in which students have conversations with classmates they have not yet met, focusing, in particular, on how to end the conversations.

Keeping a conversation going. Another aspect of conversational interaction that is useful to focus on in the language learning classroom is the strategies language learners might use to keep a conversation going. These strategies include adding extra information to a response and using follow-up questions directed at the other speaker. The activity shown in figure 15 is based on Janet Holmes and Dorothy Brown's article "Developing Sociolinguistic Competence in a Second Language" (1976). (See Paltridge 1987 for suggestions on using this activity in the classroom.)

Cross-cultural awareness activities. Other useful suggestions for

---

Cross-Cultural Note

"See you later" is a way of saying "goodbye" in American English and it often does *not* mean "I'll see you later." An American woman said "See you later" to a new immigrant in the U.S., who understood it *literally*. The American said "See you later" to her friend as they were leaving an office building. The American went one way, but the immigrant friend stayed in front of the building for twenty minutes! Later she told her friend about this and was very embarrassed about the misunderstanding. This is how she remembers her first week in the U.S.

Fig. 13. A culture note: Saying goodbye in English. (From Levine et al. 1987, 133.)

focusing on spoken genres in the language learning classroom, including cross-cultural awareness activities and feedback tasks that focus on various aspects of conversations, can be found in Rod Nolasco and Lois Arthur's *Conversation* (1987).

Beyond Language: Intercultural Communication for English as a Second Language (Levine and Adelman 1982) also provides many helpful tasks that focus on developing discourse and cultural competence in the language learning classroom. The example of a set of cross-cultural questions shown in figure 16 asks students to think about discourse patterns in their own culture and in English.

John Flowerdew (1993) provides many helpful suggestions for genre-based activities that may be applied to spoken genres. He argues that the aim of a genre-based classroom should be not so much the "near-perfect mastery of one or more genres" as showing students (1) how genre analysis can be applied to a range of genres and (2) the sorts of variation that affects genres. His emphasis is on the techniques of genre analysis rather than particular results. Examples he provides include using flowchart anaylses of structural formulae, the analysis of structural

---

The ways we start and end a conversation can depend on culture. In English, if you are the person who is ending the conversation, it's usually a good idea to give a reason. Here are some examples:

- I'm sorry, but I have to go. It was nice talking to you.
- You'll have to excuse me. I need to talk to someone over there.
- It's late. I need to be going. I'll see you tomorrow.

What do you say to end a conversation in your country?

Fig. 14. A culture note: Ending a conversation in English. (From Helgesen, Brown, and Smith 1996, 7.)

Keeping a conversation going

Suggestion 1
When asked a question, answer it and then ask a question related to something in your answer: e.g.,

     Q.

A: Where do you come from?

     A.   Q.

B: Indonesia. Have you ever been there?

In pairs

A: Where do you live?

B: (continue) _____

Suggestion 2
Answer the question, give some extra information, and then ask an appropriate question: e.g.,

     Q.

A: Are you a student?

     A.   Q.

B: Yes. I'm studying engineering. What about you?

The kind of question you ask will depend to some extent on who the person is you are talking to.

In pairs
Have conversations using the above pattern. See how long you can make them last.

1. A: Where do you come from?

    B: (continue) _____

2. A: How do you like the weather in _____?

    B: (continue) _____

Suggestion 3
To keep a conversation going, you can follow your answer with extra information and/or a question. If you only give extra information, the other person can ask you about that. If you ask a question, the other person has to answer your question. It will then be their turn to keep the conversation going. Remember, if the conversation stops, add some extra information and/or a question.

In pairs
Start conversations with these questions and see how long you can keep them going:

1. A: What do you do?

    B: (continue) _____

2. A: What part of (South America, etc.) do you come from?

    B: (continue) _____

3. A: Do you have any brothers and sisters?

    B: (continue) _____

Fig. 15. Keeping a conversation going. (From Paltridge 1987, 107–8.)

Cross-Cultural Questions

Answer the following questions about your own culture and then discuss intercultural similarities and differences.

1. What does silence indicate in conversations? Does it always indicate the same thing (e.g., approval or disapproval)?
2. Is it acceptable to interrupt others? If so, when?
3. Who can criticize whom? Under what circumstances? In what manner do people make criticisms?
4. Are there different kinds of invitations extended in your culture? Do they always result in a definite commitment (e.g., "Yes, I will come on Saturday")?
5. How do people refuse invitations? Is it appropriate to insist on someone's accepting an invitation if he or she has refused several times?
6. In comparing English verbal patterns with those in your own language, have you observed any differences or similarities (e.g., in giving opinions, asking advice, praising, boasting, expressing modesty, complaining, etc.)?

Fig. 16. Cross-cultural discourse patterns. (From Levine and Adelman 1982, 39.)

formulae using color coding, matching possible utterances to structural slots, paraphrasing and gap-filling structural slots.

Using flowchart analyses of structural formulae, highlighting possible variation. In this activity, students analyze the discourse structure of a number of instances of a genre and use their analysis to create a flowchart representation of the organization of the text. The flowchart should take account of the variation students observe between instances of the particular genre.

Analysis of structural formulae using color coding. This exercise is similar to Swales's activity using color-coded texts referred to under "Focusing on Written Genres." "Marking-up" activities are useful for identifying repetition and sequencing of structural components of texts and can be used as preparation for drawing up a flowchart illustration of the typical discourse structure of a particular genre.

Matching possible utterances to structural slots in structural formulae. In this activity, students match possible utterances to structural slots in a structural description of a particular genre. This activity can be used for both spoken and written texts. Samples of authentic spoken data, such as those provided by Ronald Carter and Michael McCarthy in *Exploring Spoken English* (1997), can be used as the basis for this kind of task. Alternatively, authentic examples of written genres can be used for this activity.

Paraphrasing. In this activity, students provide alternative encodings for particular structural slots in a genre. This task reinforces for students that there is more than one way of saying or writing the same thing, even within a single communicative context. It can also provide a context for introducing comparisons of culture-specific ways of using language.

Gap filling structural slots. In this activity, a section of a text is left out and students have to fill it in by considering what went before, what follows, and what would most likely be said in the particular section of the text.

John Flowerdew also discusses a number of metacommunication tasks in which learners analyze and discuss a piece of discourse (1993). Examples of metacommunicating include glossing the stages of a text in functional terms, examining prototypical and specialist instances of genres, and using the results of genre analysis.

Glossing the stages of a text in functional terms. In this activity, students explain what each stage of the text is aiming "to do." It is important to note, for this particular activity, that the purpose of each stage of a text is normally much more than a paraphrase of the label given to it in the text's overall generic structure.

Examining prototypical and specialist instances of genres. In this activity, students are given a collection of texts from a range of different genres and are asked to sort them into genre categories. They then choose one particular genre for study and prepare a description of the genre according to, for example, communicative purpose, audience, authority of the writer, key organizational features, key grammatical features, and key vocabulary features. Students present this description to the class, explaining which text they consider to be the most prototypically representative instance of the particular genre they chose and why. It is helpful in this task to ask students to consider both the linguistic and the nonlinguistic text features that they used for making their decision about the representativeness of the particular texts they examined.

Using the results of genre analysis. Classroom activities can also usefully draw on published results of genre analysis. This is as useful for spoken texts as it is for written ones. The guided conversation shown in figure 17 is based on Barbara Horvath and Suzanne Eggins's (1995) analysis of the discourse structure of opinion texts. The activity comes from a lesson that commenced with lead-in activities on opinion texts, listening exercises that focused on authentic opinion texts, and various language and culture-related exercises. The guided conversation was then followed by less-guided speaking activities, discussions, and open conversations in which the content, as well as the structure of the conversations, was less directed. The conversation framework was presented to the group of learners as one possible example of an opinion

Giving options: A conversation framework

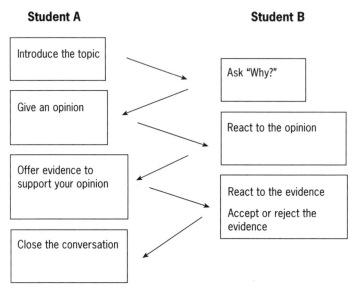

Fig. 17. A guided conversation: Opinion texts

text, rather than as a model they were required to follow. It was also stressed that students could repeat each of the opinion-related discourse elements as they wished. Learners were given the conversation framework and a pack of opinion cards, which contained various statements to use as the basis for their conversations. In pairs, students took turns picking a card, introducing the topic, and giving the opinion written on the card. Guided conversation then followed. The learners continued until they had practiced conversations for all the cards.

Clearly, activities such as these do not always produce natural conversations. They do, however, provide a framework for students to use, in combination with other aspects of genre knowledge, as a "scaffold" for their own freer and more spontaneous interactions.

Other Activities

Other activities that aim to build an awareness of how spoken genres are organized at the discourse level include

- giving students jumbled pictures that illustrate the main events in a story and asking the students to sequence the pictures while or after listening to an oral version of the story (then having students relisten to check their answers)

- asking students to match written sections of a spoken text to a flow-chart representation of the text's generic structure
- giving students completion exercises—for example, letting students listen to the beginning of a taped interaction and asking them to predict what is coming next (then having students relisten to check their answers)
- asking students to fill in charts or diagrams that focus on the discourse structure of a particular genre
- giving students information transfer activities that involve students representing the content of the genre in chart form
- asking students to listen to a tape of an interaction for particular discourse-level features, such as the way the interaction opens and closes
- asking students to listen to a tape of an interaction for ways people perform particular functions, such as ordering food in a restaurant or checking information
- giving students the tapescript of an authentic spoken text and asking them to mark the stages in the text
- asking students to observe different ways of opening and closing genres in authentic real-life situations
- asking students to observe/listen to real-life interactions to note particular features, such as how often and when someone says "please" and "thank you" or how someone changes a topic
- asking students to listen for particular adjacency pairs in a spoken interaction and to note how they were expressed
- asking students to suggest different ways in which particular structural slots can be filled—for example, different ways of closing a telephone conversation
- asking students to compare spoken and written accounts of the same event
- asking students to compare the discourse structure of a particular genre in English with the same genre in the students' first language
- having students focus on specific linguistic devices used for particular discourse-level purposes, such as "Anyway . . ." to change a topic
- having students focus on the way native speakers begin, develop, or introduce a new topic and the way they use language to do this
- having students discuss cultural differences for taking, maintaining, and giving up a turn in a conversation
- having students observe samples of natural or videotaped interactions

to focus on discourse-level strategies used by native speakers, then having students compare these interactions with the students' own role-played performances

Points to Consider

There are a number of points to remember when dealing with genres in the language learning classroom (Johns 1994). The first of these is that teachers should begin activities of genre analysis with "known texts," moving on to "unknown texts" only when students are familiar with the basic principles and techniques of genre analysis. Teachers should always aim to use texts that experts view as being representative samples of the particular genre. Teachers should consult expert users of the genre about the purpose of a text, as well as its form and style, and about how the genre might be changing. Teachers should also be sure to contextualize texts; that is, teachers should make it clear to students that texts exist in and for communities of readers and writers. Finally, teachers should always be sure to remind students that there are reasons beyond the text for the linguistic choices that people make.

Tasks and Discussion Questions

1. Genre and discourse, part 1

Analyze the following outgoing and incoming messages from a telephone answering machine to identify their generic structure. For your analysis, use the following categories: apology, undertaking, closing, identification, instruction.

Outgoing: Hello. You have rung 555-1445. I'm sorry we can't come to the phone at the moment, but if you'd like to leave your name and telephone number, we'll get back to you as soon as we can. Please leave your message after the tone. Thank you.

Incoming: Hello, Nicky. It's Sarah. Look . . . um . . . I'm trying to organize a barbecue down by the river on Friday for

Sam's fiftieth birthday. So, if you want to . . . give me a call. Bye!

Obtain several more examples of messages from telephone answering machines to analyze and add to your analysis. Think of how you might use the results of your analysis in a language learning classroom.

2. Genre and discourse, part 2

Michael McCarthy and Ronald Carter, in their book *Language as Discourse: Perspectives for Language Teaching* (1994, 33–34), gloss the stages of a narrative as follows:

Abstract	What is the story going to be about?
Orientation	Who are the participants?
	When and where did the action take place?
	In what circumstances?
Complicating action	Then what happened?
	What problems occurred?
Evaluation	What is the point of the story? So what?
Resolution	How did events sort themselves out?
	What finally happened?
Coda	What is the bridge between the events in the story and the present situation of the narrative?

Obtain examples of a spoken and written narrative and analyze them to see how well they fit this suggested discourse structure. How might you use McCarthy and Carter's framework and your sample texts in a language learning classroom?

3. Genre and casual conversation

Design an observation task in which students observe native speaker performance of casual conversations. See Rod Nolasco and Lois Arthur's book *Conversation* (1987) for suggestions on how you could do this. If you are presently teaching, ask a group of students to carry out the task and to bring the results of their observations back to the classroom for discussion. Ask your students to comment on how useful they found this activity.

4. Cross-cultural comparisons

Collect several examples of the same genre in English and another language. Analyze each text in terms of its generic structure. Check your analysis, if possible, with a native speaker of whichever of the languages is not your first language. If the texts you have chosen are in a specialized subject area, check your analysis with someone who knows the subject area well. Consider the texts in terms of similarities and differences in move patterns. Ask your native speaker informants if they are able to offer any explanation for what you have observed.

5. A classroom application

Choose a text that is suitable for a particular group of students and analyze it in terms of its generic structure, text structure, or moves. Then develop activities choosing from the suggestions presented in this chapter for language practice activities that focus on discourse awareness and skills. Plan a lesson that uses these activities.

Further Reading

Bhatia, V. K. 1993. *Analysing Genre: Language Use in Professional Settings.* London: Longman. See chapter 6, "From Description to Explanation in Language Teaching."

Connor, U. 1996. *Contrastive Rhetoric: Cross-Cultural Aspects of Second Language Writing.* Cambridge: Cambridge University Press. See chapter 8, "Genre-Specific Studies in Contrastive Rhetoric."

Cook, G. 1989. *Discourse.* Oxford: Oxford University Press. See chapter 10, "Managing Conversation"; chapter 12, "Developing Discourse in the Classroom."

Cox, L. 1998. A genre to remember. In P. Master and D. Brinton, eds., *New Ways in English for Specific Purposes.* Alexandria, VA: TESOL.

Flowerdew, J. 1993. An educational, or process, approach to the teaching of professional genres. *ELT Journal* 47 (4): 305–16.

Nolasco, R., and L. Arthur. 1987. *Conversation.* Oxford: Oxford University Press.

Olsher, D. 1998. How's your genre awareness? In P. Master and D. Brinton, eds., *New Ways in English for Specific Purposes.* Alexandria, VA: TESOL.

Orr, T. 1998. Creating lifetime genre files. In P. Master and D. Brinton, eds., *New Ways in English for Specific Purposes.* Alexandria, VA: TESOL.

Paltridge, B. 1996. Genre, text type, and the language learning classroom. *ELT Journal* 50 (3): 237–43.

Paltridge, B. 2002. Genre, text type, and the EAP classroom. In A. Johns, ed., *Genre and the Classroom: Multiple Perspectives.* Mahwah, NJ: Lawrence Erlbaum.

Riggenbach, H. 1999. *Discourse Analysis in the Language Classroom.* Vol. 1, *The Spoken Language.* Ann Arbor: University of Michigan Press. See chapter 3, "Ways of Speaking."

Chapter 5

Genre and Language

There are a number of views on the nature of genre-specific language. Tom Hutchinson and Alan Waters, in their book *English for Specific Purposes: A Learning-Centred Approach* (1987), for example, make a distinction between the language of an area of specialization (e.g., medicine or tourism) and the language of the genres found in these particular areas. In their view, no grammatical structure or function or discourse structure can be identified with any particular subject. They argue that the main way in which language varies between areas of specialization is in the use of technical and specialized vocabulary.

More recent developments in the area of corpus studies, however, are starting to reveal that there is support for the notion of language for specific purposes, as well as for genre-specific language. The picture might, however, be more complex than has previously been thought. Douglas Biber (1988), for example, in his corpus-based study, found a wide range of linguistic variation within the particular genres examined, some of which he describes as surprising and contrary to popular expectation. His conclusion is that different kinds of text are complex in different ways and that many earlier conclusions that have been reached about language for specific purposes reflect our incomplete understanding of the linguistic characteristics of discourse complexity (Biber 1992). In his view, there clearly are language differences between genres. These differences, however, can only be revealed through the examination of actual texts rather than through any intuitions we may have about them. This is an area where ESP genre studies have already devoted a great amount of attention, from early studies of frequency to more recent studies of the language of academic and professional genres.

An important early study of genre-specific language is Elaine Tarone and her colleagues' examination of the use of the passive in astrophysics journal articles (Tarone et al. 1981). Although they only examined two sample texts, they found that, in contrast with the results of previous frequency studies that combine texts from a range of scientific fields, the texts they examined used *we* + an active verb (e.g., "In the paper, we discuss . . .") as often as the passive (e.g., "it was pointed out that . . ."). As a result of discussions they had with a specialist informant, they found, however, that *we* + active, on the one hand, and the passive, on the other, perform quite different functions in the texts they examined. For example, *we* + active was used to indicate the particular method an author chose for the study, whereas the passive was used to indicate more standard, or established, procedures. They also found that authors used *we* + active to describe their own work and used the passive to describe the work of other researchers. An important aspect of the study by Tarone and her colleagues is thus the use of a specialist informant to help them find an explanation for what they observed in their analysis and description.

It is important, then, to incorporate ethnographic information, or "insiders' views," into genre-based descriptions of language use. Esther Ramani and her colleagues found, for example, that in their teaching of the conventions of citation and referencing to doctoral students, they were forced to abandon developing a universal style guide for all doctoral students in their institution, as most research groups, they discovered, had their own conventions that they were reluctant to change. Instead, in the experience of Ramani and her colleagues, it became more worthwhile to encourage students to look at theses recently completed in their own areas of specialization to find out exactly how they were expected to refer to previous research (Ramani et al. 1988).

The work in both ESP and the systemic genre field provides many examples of teaching genre-specific language. *Academic Writing for Graduate Students: Essential Tasks and Skills* (Swales and Feak 1994), for example, includes exercises that focus on such aspects of language as linking words, *-ing* clauses of result, linking *as* clauses, prepositions of time, nominal *that* clauses, unreal conditionals, special verb agreements, hyphens in noun phrases, claiming centrality, citation and tense choice, negative openings, and tense and purpose statements. *Writing Up Research: Experimental Report Writing for Students of English* (Weissberg and Buker 1990) includes tasks that focus on general and specific noun phrases, word repetition and derivation, citation focus and verb tense, attitude and tense in reporting findings, signal words and verb tense, tense and voice in descriptions of materials and procedures, and verb tense in commenting on results.

A detailed discussion of genre-specific language is also provided in Peter Knapp and Meg Watkins's *Context—Text—Grammar: Teaching the Genres and Grammar of School Writing in Infants and Primary Classrooms* (1994). Their book's section on genre-based grammar provides a helpful comparison of functional and "traditional" grammar, discourse-level grammar, sentence-level grammar, and grammar at the level of words. Knapp and Watkins provide detailed grammatical descriptions of explanations, instructions, descriptions, arguments, and narratives, as well as examples of how they have found it useful to focus on these in the language learning classroom (see "A Genre-Based Grammar" later in the present chapter).

Examples of analyses of grammatical patterns typical of anecdotes, descriptions, expositions, news items, procedures, recounts, reports, and reviews are provided in *English for Social Purposes: A Handbook for Teachers of Adult Literacy* (Hammond et al. 1992). This book also includes examples of units of work that include a focus on patterns of grammar and vocabulary within the context of genre-based instruction.

Grammar is often taught in such a way that it is not always easy for learners to relate what they are studying to their overall learning purpose (Humphrey 1990). Grammar is also often taught through sentence-based examples rather than through whole texts (Celce-Murcia and Olshtain 2000). A focus on grammar in a genre-based classroom aims to link the teaching of language to learning purpose by focusing on language within the context of the genres students need to perform. *Academic Writing for Graduate Students* (Swales and Feak 1994) and *Writing Up Research* (Weissberg and Buker 1990) are clear examples of this approach, as is the systemic classroom-based genre work. In both of these strands of work, the focus on grammar and meaning occurs within the context of learning particular genres, rather than outside of them. The examination of sample texts aims to explore not only how but also why particular language features occur (Mackay 1995).

A genre-based classroom also provides a context for the examination of rhetorical strategies within the context of learning particular genres; that is, it provides a context for examining the choices writers and speakers make to convince readers and listeners of their claims, as well as the ways speakers and writers adapt to their audiences (Mauranen 1993). This might include examining the ways speakers and writers present arguments; the circumstances in which they "hedge," or use vague language; or the way they cite other sources to give authority to their texts.

Genre and Spoken and Written Language

One aspect of language use that can be explored in genre-based classrooms is the differences between spoken and written language. This aspect lends itself well to genre-based instruction, as most genres that students need to learn are normally either spoken or written and much less often both.

It is useful to consider this *spoken-written continuum* in lesson planning and teaching. Joyce (1992) suggests planning series of activities that move progressively from spoken to written texts, drawing learners' attention to the spoken or written characteristics of the genre she is focusing on as she goes. Spoken and written language play equally important but different roles in education (Hammond et al. 1992). Students need to have an understanding of what is characteristic of the genre they are studying being a spoken or a written text as much as they need to know about other linguistic (and nonlinguistic) aspects of the particular genre.

Some authors have suggested that written language is more structurally complex and elaborate than spoken language. Others have suggested that speech might be more structurally complex than writing. For example, Michael Halliday, in his book *Spoken and Written Language* (1989), presents the notion of *grammatical intricacy* to account for the way that the relationship between clauses can be much more spread out in spoken language than in written language. These relationships can also be extremely complex. For example, the following sentence is made up of ten clauses, each of which has a particular relationship with another clause in the overall *clause complex.*

I can't mind the kids today
because I must go to football training
and I can't leave early
because we've got an important game on Saturday
and if we win it
we go into the finals
but Wednesday's fine
because I don't have training
so I can mind them
if that's OK with you.

(Gerot and Wignell 1994, 162)

According to Halliday, written language also tends to be more "lexically dense" than spoken language; that is, in spoken language, content tends to be spread out over a number of clauses rather than being packed into larger noun groups in one single clause. This notion of *lexical density* refers to the ratio of content words to grammatical, or function, words within a clause. Content words include nouns and verbs, while grammatical words include such things as prepositions, pronouns, and articles. Halliday (1989, 61) offers sample sentences that show how written language can be more lexically dense than spoken language. His sample written sentence contains seven content, or lexical, words (italicized) and three grammatical words.

> *Investment* in a *rail facility implies* a *long-term commitment.*

His spoken version of the same sentence contains seven content words and thirteen grammatical words.

> If you *invest* in a *rail facility,* this *implies* that you are going to be *committed* for a *long term.*

The written version is more lexically dense than the spoken one.

Lexical density is a result, in part, of the high level of *nominalization* that is typical of written texts, where actions and events are often presented as nouns rather than as verbs and so on. Thus, the spoken example

> If our meter reader can't get at your meter to read it to find out how much you owe, we'll have to estimate your account.

might be written:

> Where a reading of a meter cannot be made for the purpose of rendering an account because of the absence of access to the meter, the account may bear an estimated reading instead of the actual reading. (Gerot and Wignell 1994, 148)

Michael Halliday calls this phenomenon *grammatical metaphor,* that is, a situation where a language item is transferred from a more expected grammatical class to another. In the preceding written sentence, actions that are typically realized as verbs are realized as nouns or noun groups.

verb groups	*noun groups*
can't get at	the absence of access
to read	a reading, the actual reading
to find out	for the purpose of rendering
owe	the account
will have to estimate	an estimated reading

(Gerot and Wignell 1994, 148)

This high level of nominalization leads to much more tightly packed texts in terms of information content in written texts and to a lower lexical load in spoken texts. For this reason, such spoken texts as the news can be difficult for language learners to understand, as they are really examples of written language being spoken. Other examples of written texts being spoken often include lectures and conference presentations and are often equally difficult for language learners to follow.

In "more written" texts, language is more often used as reflection rather than to accompany action as is the case with some "more spoken" texts (e.g., the language that accompanies games and sports). In other cases, such as plays and political speeches, texts are written to sound like speaking and so have more in common with spoken texts than with written texts (Hammond et al. 1992). Spoken language also tends to be more dependent on the context in which it occurs than is written language.

Thus, written language is not just speech written down. Speaking and writing draw on the same underlying grammatical system but, in general, encode meanings in different ways depending on what they wish to represent. The difference between spoken and written language can be presented as a continuum with the extremes showing marked differences but with points close together being quite similar. The continuum shown in figure 18 summarizes this view.

The corpus-based work carried out by Douglas Biber supports this notion of a spoken-written language continuum. His work shows that there are no absolute characteristics of written or spoken language, that spoken and written language are, rather, "multidimensional constructs," with some spoken and written genres having features in common with other spoken and written genres and also having characteristics that show them to be quite different (Biber 1988).

Spoken language also contains more half-completed and reformulated utterances than does written language. Another characteristic of spoken language is the use of fillers, such as "mhm" and "ah" and "you know." Spoken language is normally produced "on-line," whereas there

Fig. 18. The spoken-written language continuum. (From Gerot and Wignell 1994, 161.)

is normally more time for the production of written language. With spoken language, topics can also be changed "on-line"; speakers can interrupt and overlap each other. Speakers can ask for clarification and correct what they said, so that misunderstandings can be cleared up immediately. Spoken language also uses much more repetition, hesitation, and redundancy than does written language. Also, spoken language is able to use intonation, gesture, body language, and so forth to convey meaning, whereas ways of conveying meaning are much more limited in written language. Table 4 summarizes these and other characteristics of spoken and written language.

There are, however, important similarities between spoken language and written language. Both are similar in that, as with any act of communication, they must take account of their audiences. Both speakers and writers need to consider what other participants already know about the topic, what has already been expressed in the discourse, and role relationships between participants in the communication. They also need to make it as easy as possible for their listeners or readers to interpret correctly what they say.

A Genre-Based Grammar

A genre-based view of grammar focuses on language at the level of whole text and at the same time takes into account ways in which meanings are expressed at the level of grammar and vocabulary. It also examines the stages through which a text moves to achieve its particular goal. Classroom applications of this view of language focus on both text and context and discuss discourse, vocabulary choice, and grammar in relation to them. Figure 19 presents Peter Knapp and Meg Watkins's (1994) proposal for a genre-based view of grammar.

TABLE 4. Some Differences between Spoken and Written Language

Spoken Language	Written Language
Hearer present (usually)	Reader (usually) not present at the time of writing
Ways of conveying meaning beyond syntax and vocabulary are more varied (e.g., intonation, gesture, body language, etc.)	Ways of conveying meaning beyond syntax and vocabulary are limited to certain orthographic conventions (e.g., paragraphing, formatting, headings, use of illustrations, etc.)
Nonlinguistic aspects of the immediate setting can be important to the interpretation of meaning (e.g., "There it is")	Immediate setting is normally irrelevant to the interpretation of meaning (in that we can read the newspaper on the bus, at the breakfast table, etc.)
Use of fillers, repetition, hesitations, and redundancy	Much less repetition and redundancy Hesitation may be expressed in a different way (e.g., by using certain lexical items to "hedge")
Use of incomplete utterances	Usually complete sentences
Lexically sparse (fewer content words)	Lexically dense (more content words)
More complex relations between clauses	Less complex relations between clauses
More immediate feedback	Less immediate feedback
Language is normally produced "on-line"	More time for the production of language
Topic can be changed "on-line"	
Speakers can interrupt and overlap with each other	
Speakers can ask for clarification "on-line"	
Speakers can correct what they said	
Speakers can clear up misunderstandings immediately	

At the text level, a teacher might choose to focus on the visual layout of a text, its generic structure, the thematic structure of the text (i.e., the way the *theme,* or beginning point of the clause, might pick up, or repeat, an item from a preceding clause), or ways in which the text (in the case of written texts) is broken up into paragraphs. Other text-level aspects of language use that might be considered include patterns of cohesion, such as reference and conjunction.

Sentence-level aspects that might be focused on include verb and noun choices and the organization of clauses. Noun groups might also be examined—in particular, the use of pronouns, the use of determiners (e.g., articles), and the use of other nouns or adjectives to modify the main noun of a nominal group. Other aspects that might be considered include the ways in which we use *modality* (e.g., the use of such items as

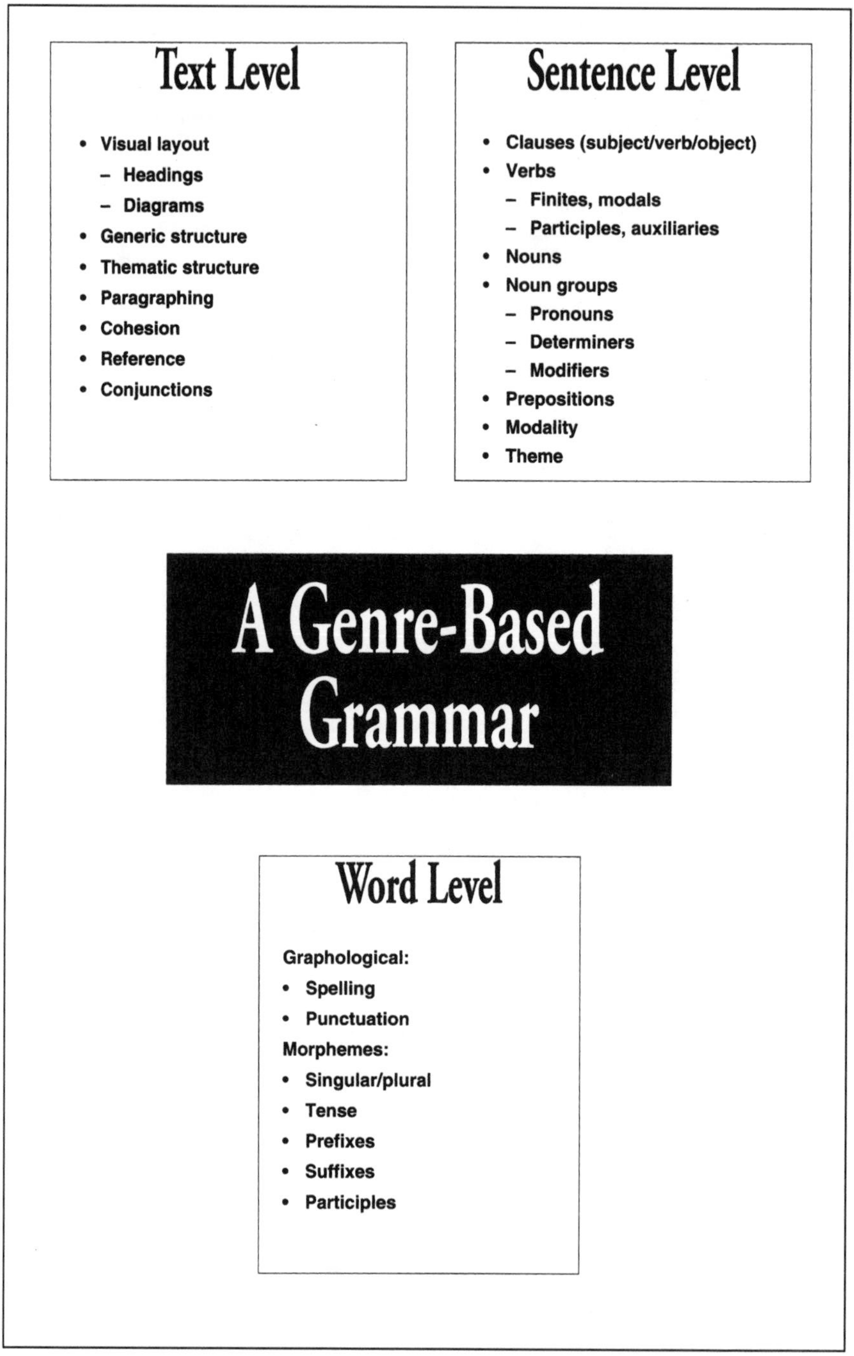

Text Level

- Visual layout
  - Headings
  - Diagrams
- Generic structure
- Thematic structure
- Paragraphing
- Cohesion
- Reference
- Conjunctions

Sentence Level

- Clauses (subject/verb/object)
- Verbs
  - Finites, modals
  - Participles, auxiliaries
- Nouns
- Noun groups
  - Pronouns
  - Determiners
  - Modifiers
- Prepositions
- Modality
- Theme

A Genre-Based Grammar

Word Level

Graphological:
- Spelling
- Punctuation

Morphemes:
- Singular/plural
- Tense
- Prefixes
- Suffixes
- Participles

Fig. 19. A genre-based grammar. (From Knapp and Watkins 1994, 33.)

"might," "will," "can," "possibly," and "perhaps") to qualify what we say. Students might also be asked to consider the "point of departure," or theme, of clauses—that is, in Michael Halliday's (1994) terms, what the clause is "about." Students can also be asked to consider where new information is presented in the clause and where the writer or speaker places what the audience already knows.

At the word level, a teacher might choose to focus on spelling and punctuation (in written texts) and on the structure of words, such as ways in which plurals and past tense participles are formed. It is also useful for language learners to understand the use of prefixes and suffixes to change the meaning of words.

Activities That Focus on Language Awareness and Skills

An important decision teachers have to make is what aspects of language they should draw attention to in their course of instruction. They may choose to focus on aspects of phonology, such as stress, intonation, rhythm, or individual sounds. They may, equally, wish to draw learners' attention to certain genre-specific grammatical features. The relationship between language items may also be given attention by examining patterns of cohesion in sample texts. The ways in which language functions are expressed, sociocultural norms and conventions, and paralinguistic features of communication (e.g., signs and gestures) may also be given attention. The important question to be asked is how this can be done in a way that maintains the discourse-level perspective on language analysis and use that is an inherent part of a genre-based language learning program.

The following section summarizes a number of approaches to focusing on language in relation to whole texts, or genres, and specific contexts of use. The important point in each of these approaches is to focus on the use of language in relation to its particular context of use and in relation to the other language that surrounds it, rather than on decontextualized, isolated examples of language use.

Sometimes a whole-text approach to language analysis seems to be the only way of making sense of certain grammatical items (Conway and Thaine 1997). Teachers need to analyze the interaction of grammar and discourse and then teach both discourse and grammar in appropriate ways to language learners (Celce-Murcia 1990, 1996; Celce-Murcia and Olshtain 2000). The key to doing this is to base classroom materials on authentic samples of discourse that are appropriate both to the learners' proficiency level and to their interests and needs. In Celce-Murcia's view, a sentence-based knowledge of grammar is necessary, but not sufficient (1990). It needs to be combined with an analysis of grammar drawn from authentic, whole texts.

Teacher-prepared texts can be useful, particularly at the beginning stages of language learning. However, as students gain in proficiency, they need to be introduced to language that reflects the way native speakers use English outside the classroom (Burns and Joyce 1997). Many teachers try to create "authentic-like" situations in the classroom, whereas, in reality, the language students meet outside the classroom is often much more challenging and quite different from what they have met in class. In the view of Burns and Joyce, if the overall aim of a program is to prepare students to use language effectively in real-life situations, teachers need to present students with authentic texts in the classroom and to base the language work they do with their students on these texts.

Using authentic listening or reading materials. Learners' attention may be drawn to language through the use of authentic listening or reading materials. The particular language sample chosen needs to be selected with the learners' proficiency level, needs, and interests in mind. The text chosen may initially be dealt with as it would in any work on receptive skills, with appropriate prelistening (or prereading) and postlistening (or postreading) activities. A particular language feature may then be highlighted in the text and focused on for the purposes of instruction. This approach lends itself particularly well to a genre-based perspective in that it provides real-life examples of language in specific contexts of use.

Guided discovery. In activities of guided discovery, teachers may choose to lead from an example to a rule, or they may design activities for learners to work out the rules for themselves. They may use preview activities in which learners are instructed to go through a text and find as many examples of a particular language feature as they can. Students are then asked to decide whether all uses of the particular language feature have the same meaning and to describe the ways in which uses that do not have the same meaning are different.

Matching techniques are another useful language learning activity employing guided discovery. For example, learners might be asked to join halves of sentences, such as the component parts of tag questions and conditionals, taken from an authentic sample of language use.

Matching techniques are also useful for highlighting the use of discourse markers and conjunctions in texts.

Learners might also be asked to compare and contrast grammatical structures. For example, they could be asked to compare "John ate the ice cream and he liked it" and "John ate the ice cream because he liked it" (Celce-Murcia 1990, 137) and to establish the difference in meaning between the sentences. From that, they then work out a rule.

Another approach is for learners to study a text for examples of particular language forms and then group them according to some common feature. This kind of activity is suitable, for example, for focusing on countable and uncountable nouns, the use of articles, word order, verb choices, and certain features of pronunciation. Learners may, for example, look for instances of the simple past (in English) in a text and group them according to pronunciation of the final /s/ morpheme. Or they may be asked to find all the uses of the present perfect and put them into groups on the basis of differences in meanings expressed.

Feedback on performance. Another approach increasingly being used in language learning classrooms is often called *test-teach-test,* or *feedback on performance.* In this approach, the teacher puts learners in a communicative situation in which they are required to use language to complete a task. The teacher then monitors the learners' performance and provides input in response to any specific difficulties the learners may have had. Such an approach is clearly demanding in terms of resources and the teacher's (instant) language knowledge. It does, however, have the important advantage that it focuses on and responds to students' immediate language learning needs.

Using native speaker models. In a variation of the approach that utilizes feedback on performance, students perform a task, then the teacher provides the students with a native speaker model of that task. Students compare their performance with the native speaker model, analyze differences, and then repeat the task, incorporating the differences they have identified between their own and the native speaker's performances of the task.

Explaining. Language features may also be explained to learners. An important consideration here is how a "rule" may be stated to learners so that it is both accessible and useful to them. Consideration also needs to be given as to how the rule might best be presented on the board, how the use of the rule might be demonstrated, and how learners' understanding of the concept, form, and meaning of the particular language feature might be checked.

Grammatical consciousness raising. An approach that has received increased attention recently is grammatical consciousness raising (Ellis 1992). This approach is based on the position that the acquisition of implicit language knowledge involves three processes:

1. Noticing: learners become conscious of the presence of a linguistic feature in the input, whereas previously they had ignored it.
2. Comparing: learners compare the linguistic feature noticed in the input with their own mental grammar, registering to what extent there is a "gap" between the input and their grammar.
3. Integrating: learners integrate a representation of the new linguistic feature into their mental grammar.

Grammatical consciousness raising thus facilitates the acquisition of the grammatical knowledge needed for communication. Activities of grammatical consciousness raising, like activities of guided discovery, involve tasks that help learners construct their own explicit grammar (Ellis 1993).

A lesson that incorporates grammatical consciousness raising may commence with a focus on language through a text and then be followed by consciousness-raising tasks that focus on particular grammatical rules or concepts. For example, learners might be asked to find examples of particular language features in a text and to identify similarities and/or differences in their meaning and use. Learners might also be asked to translate forms into and out of their first language and to identify similarities and differences in use, form, or concept.

Interpretation grammar activities. Rod Ellis (1992) also suggests the use of what he calls *interpretation grammar activities.* These activities involve providing learners with input that contains a particular language feature and asking them to identify the meaning of the language item in the particular context. Learners thus listen to input and interpret, rather than produce, language.

Assessing field, tenor, and mode. John Flowerdew (1993) suggests an activity in which students consider what in the text relates to the particular topic (field), what indicates particular role relationships (tenor), and what seems to be characteristic of the text being a spoken or written text (mode). He points out that it is not necessary to actually use the terms *field, tenor,* and *mode* with students. These categories are, nonetheless, useful to keep in mind when asking students to examine how aspects of the "context of situation" impact the language used in a particular text.

Role-play focusing on variation in field, tenor, or mode. In this activity, students role-play a particular activity but with a change in the topic (field) of the interaction, the relationship between participants (tenor), or the mode (e.g., a written text might be used as the basis for a spoken interaction).

Concordancing. John Flowerdew also suggests the use of concordancing activities in the language learning classroom. In these activities, students examine a number of instances of a particular genre, or two different genres, looking for the use of particular language features in the texts, such as (1) the way in which the word *say* might be used to report rather than quote or (2) ways of reporting in academic texts.

Language Practice Activities

Once learners' attention has been drawn to particular language features, learners may then be provided with opportunities to use the language, in what Rod Ellis (1993) calls *focused communication activities.* Penny Ur's book *Grammar Practice Activities* (1988) provides an excellent collection of such activities, as do Friederike Klippel's *Keep Talking* (1984) and Rod Nolasco and Lois Arthur's *Conversation* (1987). Martin Bygate's *Speaking* (1987), Tricia Hedge's *Writing* (1988), and Christopher Tribble's *Writing* (1996) also provide many excellent examples of language practice activities that can be used in a genre-based language learning program.

Examples of speaking practice activities include

- information gap activities where each student has a different set of information and the students ask each other questions to obtain a complete set of the information
- questionnaires and surveys where students question each other or people outside the classroom to find out something they do not already know
- communication games that focus on key aspects of language use (see, e.g., Jill Hadfield's books *Elementary Communication Games* [1984], *Intermediate Communication Games* [1990], and *Advanced Communication Games* [1987])
- controlled language practice activities that focus on key aspects of language (see, e.g., Ur 1988)
- drills that focus on the aspects of language highlighted in a lesson
- personalization activities in which students use language they have just studied to tell someone something about themselves or about something they know

- activities in which learners observe and aim to replicate native speaker language use
- fluency activities that aim to encourage the use of certain language features (see, e.g., Klippel 1984; Nolasco and Arthur 1987)
- ranking activities in which students are given a list of items to prioritize
- "jigsaw" activities where each student has a different set of information and the students combine their information to complete a task
- role-play activities in which students take on particular roles to practice a language feature highlighted in a lesson
- consensus activities in which students are given a problem to solve and must do so by reaching agreement with each other
- problem-solving activities in which students are given a problem to solve, with or without each other's agreement
- retelling activities in which students retell to other students something they have just heard or read about
- postlistening/postreading discussions in which students discuss some aspect of the subject matter of the lesson
- feedback activities in which students look closely at their own language use and aim to improve their performance (see Nolasco and Arthur 1987)

Examples of writing practice activities include

- controlled writing tasks, such as (1) gap filling with or without given alternatives and (2) linking sentences choosing from a range of given alternative language items
- composing activities, such as prewriting, rewriting, and editing tasks (see Hedge 1988)
- activities that focus on putting pieces of a text together and on developing ideas within the overall structure of the text
- audience-oriented tasks that focus on writing for a particular reader
- parallel writing activities where students write a text similar to the one focused on in the lesson but substitute words or phrases of their own, or they may rework a model text with a change in topic or in the relationship between writer and audience
- guided writing activities where a paragraph or whole text is constructed from a supplied set of notes
- cued writing activities where students

write a text on the basis of a structural outline presented earlier in a lesson write a text using the first paragraph of the text as a stimulus and a set of notes for the rest of the text

write a text on the basis of a given set of key words

rewrite a passage from a different point of view

write a shorter version of a text

write a text from a set of instructions (e.g., writing a letter applying for a job based on a job advertisement and position description)

write a text from a picture sequence

write the middle section of a text after having been given its beginning and ending sections

- activities where students take notes and summarize an oral text as if, for example, taking minutes at a meeting or listening to a lecture
- writing tasks where students write their own independent text based on the content of a lesson
- improving activities, such as responding to teacher feedback, re-drafting, and postwriting checking and editing (see Hedge 1988)

It is important that focused communication activities provide a context in which the language features and skills they are intended to practice might reasonably arise. The activities should also maximize student practice opportunities, rather than require an overly long amount of preparation or classroom management time. Teachers should, however, be sure to help and guide students in the performance of the tasks, to increase the chances of success and the effectiveness of the practice activity as a whole (Ur 1996).

It is also important that the tasks are designed for success; that is, the activities should be ones that learners are likely to succeed in doing, rather than being beyond learners' present capabilities. It is also helpful if the tasks can be performed at differing levels, so that learners with different levels of proficiency are equally challenged by the activity. Language practice activities also need to be interesting, focusing on an interesting topic, conveying meaningful information, appealing to learners' feelings, or challenging their intellect (Ur 1996).

Extension Activities

It is also important to provide extension activities that recycle the language focused on in the classroom and direct students, wherever possible, to use the language in meaningful contexts outside the classroom (Burns and Joyce 1997).

Extension activities might include

- providing students with different contexts in which to carry out similar interactions or perform similar written tasks
- increasing the length of a task the learners are required to complete
- increasing the complexity of an interaction or written task
- increasing the number of participants in an interaction
- introducing unpredictable or problematic elements into an activity
- increasing the number of outcomes that have to be achieved through an interaction or piece of writing
- introducing genre mixing into the task (e.g., mixing a service encounter with a phase of casual conversation, an argument with a letter of complaint)
- asking students to perform related tasks outside the classroom (see Burns and Joyce 1997)

Tasks and Discussion Questions

1. Spoken and written language

Analyze a text or set of texts that would be useful to examine in a language learning classroom for features that are characteristic of them being written or spoken texts. Develop language learning activities that focus on these particular features, choosing from this chapter's suggestions for activities that focus on language awareness and skills.

2. Genre-based grammar

Choose a text suitable for a group of students with which you are familiar and analyze it in terms of Peter Knapp and Meg Watkins's model for a genre-based grammar, presented in this chapter (fig. 19). Develop language learning activities that focus on the language features you have analyzed, choosing from this chapter's suggestions for activities that focus on language awareness and skills. Plan a lesson that uses these activities.

Further Reading

Batstone, R. 1994. *Grammar.* Oxford: Oxford University Press. See section 2, "Demonstration: Teaching Grammar."

Harmer, J. 1987. *Teaching and Learning Grammar.* London: Longman.

Harmer, J. 1998. *How to Teach English.* London: Longman. See chapter 6, "How to Teach Language."

Hedge, T. 2000. *Teaching and Learning in the Language Classroom.* Oxford: Oxford University Press. See chapter 5, "Grammar."

Nunan, D. 1999. *Second Language Teaching and Learning.* Boston: Heinle and Heinle. See chapter 4, "Focus on Language."

Riggenbach, H. 1999. *Discourse Analysis in the Language Classroom.* Vol. 1, *The Spoken Language.* Ann Arbor: University of Michigan Press. See chapter 4, "Micro Skills: Pronunciation, Grammar, and Vocabulary."

Thornbury, S. 1997. *About Language: Tasks for Teachers of English.* Cambridge: Cambridge University Press. See pp. 126–36, "Texts, Conversations."

Thornbury, S. 2000. *How to Teach Grammar.* London: Longman.

Ur, P. 1988. *Grammar Practice Activities.* Cambridge: Cambridge University Press.

Chapter 6

Genre-Based Assessment

Genre-based assessment has a number of advantages over more general approaches to language assessment. The first advantage is that students bring their knowledge of the purpose, structure, and grammatical characteristics of genres to the assessment situation in a way that helps them deal with unfamiliar content and vocabulary in the testing material. Further, the relevance of the assessment material to the learners' goals ensures a more accurate assessment of their ability to operate in a target environment, making the assessment a better predictor of student success. The use of genuine, authentic, and relevant examples of genres in the assessment situation ensures less of a gap between assessment material and students' real-life target situations (Bhatia 1993).

Assessment of second language writing, in particular, needs to be increasingly concerned with genre (Fulcher 1998). If genres are culturally conditioned and institutionalized and can be recognized and classified from their communicative purpose, second language assessment, in his view, needs to account for this. Genre-based assessment is especially relevant, he suggests, where a learner's target performance needs can be identified with some degree of certainty. This is particularly the case in ESP settings, such as academic and business English courses, but also in other settings where the genres being focused on are genres that students need to be able to understand and use.

Principles of Genre-Based Assessment

There are many helpful suggestions for genre-based assessment in the systemic genre work. Six key principles underlie this work. These principles are discussed by Mary Macken and Diana Slade in their essay "Assessment: A Foundation for Effective Learning in the School Context" (1993).

1. Learners should know that, at some stage, they will be assessed.
2. The assessment criteria being used should be made explicit to learners; that is, the criteria should be explained to students in terms and at a level that they will understand.
3. The assessment method and ratings that will be used should be explained to learners in language that is adapted to their level. Students should be aware how the assessment will be carried out and what aspects of their performance will be focused on.
4. The assessment should be related to the aims and objectives of the program students are undertaking or the purpose for which students are taking the test.
5. The assessment should be reliable and valid. Thus, there should be some level of assessor training aimed at consistent and agreed on ratings among assessors. Also, the assessment tasks should assess what they aim to access. For example, an oral interview should not be used to assess whether a student is capable of carrying out particular writing tasks.
6. The assessment should be reported in terms that are common to teachers, curriculum writers, and program managers; that is, the assessment should use descriptions that are common to and shared by each of the potential users of the results of the assessment.

Examples of Genre-Based Assessment

The New South Wales Adult Migrant Education Service's *Certificate in Spoken and Written English* (Hagan et al. 1993) uses the notion of competencies as the basis for its genre-based framework for the design of language learning programs and the assessment of learner outcomes. These competencies describe what a learner should be able to do at the end of a particular course. Each of the competencies is described in terms of such elements as purpose, discourse structure, grammar, vocabulary, and phonology. Table 5 shows the competency statement for learners who "can recount a short familiar event." This competency statement is written to be used in an Australian classroom but can easily be adapted for use in other teaching settings.

Peter Knapp and Meg Watkins (1994) also provide helpful examples of genre-based assessment. Their "story plan" for narratives (shown in fig. 20) can be used both for scaffolding spoken and written texts and for assessing them.

TABLE 5. A Competency Statement: Can Recount a Short Familiar Event

Elements	Performance Criteria	Range of Variables	Examples of Texts/ Assessment Tasks
Purpose i. has knowledge of purpose of text and can recount a short, familiar event	• outline of events in recount is understood by interlocutor	• face to face • small group	**Texts** • Recounts of events, e.g., weekend activities • Experience stories
Discourse Structure ii. can produce appropriate staging iii. can relate past events to produce a short coherent text iv. can manage some conversational techniques where required	• produces appropriate text staging • relates past events • uses minimal conversational techniques, e.g., asking for clarification, repetition, challenging (verbally or nonverbally) where required	• interlocutor has experience with NESB speakers • limited amount of information—approximately 1–2 minutes	
Grammar/Vocabulary v. signal the past vi. can use simple conjunctive links vii. can use appropriate key vocabulary	• uses some past time markers, e.g., attempts at past tense, "yesterday," "last week" • uses some simple conjunctive links, e.g., "first," "then" • uses key vocabulary		**Tasks** • Learners relate previous afternoon's activities • Learners give recount of journey to Australia • Learners give recount of weekend activities
Phonology viii. can produce intelligible pronunciation/stress/ intonation	• produces most intelligible pronunciation/stress/ intonation which may require interlocutor to verify		

Source: From Hagan et al. 1993, 20.

Story Plan	
Theme	
Orientation	
Character	Description
•	
•	
•	
•	
Where:	
When:	
Complications	
Events:	
•	
•	
•	
•	
•	
Reflection:	
•	
•	
Resolution	

Fig. 20. A story plan for narratives. (From Knapp and Watkins 1994, 152.)

A more general assessment grid, based on the systemic teaching and learning cycle (see my chap. 2 in the present book) to be used with different genres is shown in figure 21. A grid can be drawn up for each genre to be focused on, then individual grids can be drawn up for individual students, showing what aspects of the genre they can control and what future action needs to be taken

Observing and Assessing Spoken Genres

Recent years have seen important changes in the ways in which learners' second spoken language is reported on and assessed. In particular, increased attention has been given to the notion of communicative

Teaching Cycle	Knowledge of Social Structure	Generic Structure	Language Features	Engagement with Text/ Activities	Comments/Action
Building knowledge of field/context	• identifies social context • differentiates text from other texts • identifies social purpose of text			• talks about experiences • participates in class activities	
Modeling	• identifies social function of text • identifies types of people who write text • identifies audience for text	• identifies generic structure of text • differentiates stages of text • identifies distinctive language features related to stages	In a modeled text can identify: • • •	• employs appropriate reading strategies • participates actively in modeling activities	
Joint construction	• can discuss social function of text • can discuss characteristics of social context • can talk about relation of reader to writer	• can outline generic structure • can identify and sequence different stages of text	Contributes suggestions to construction of text using language features: • • •	• participates actively in group negotiation • employs metalanguage • can discuss reading/ writing strategies	
Independent construction	• chooses genre independently • understanding of social purpose revealed in text • understanding of reader and writer relationship	• can reproduce text structure • uses linguistic features appropriate to each stage	Text constructed through use of linguistic features: • •	• approaches text confidently • can discuss appropriate reading/writing strategies	

Fig. 21. A general assessment grid. (From Joyce 1992, 51.)

performance testing and to the notion of "evaluation as an aid to learning" (Brindley 1989, 5). Paltridge (1998) describes an approach to assessing spoken genres that aims to draw both of these concerns together. In this approach, the teacher observes and evaluates the learners' oral performance of particular genres, then provides them with detailed feedback based on specific performance-related criteria. The learners then draw on this evaluation and feedback for setting individual language learning goals.

First, the teacher chooses an oral communication task that focuses on a genre the students are presently studying. The teacher makes a copy of the observation sheet in figure 22 for each of the students in the class. The teacher sets up the communication task, then observes the learners' oral interactions pair by pair or group by group, as appropriate. The teacher makes notes about individual learners' performance according to the categories on the observation schedule, using the performance criteria from table 6 as the basis for the comments she or he writes on the observation sheets. The teacher provides a general feedback session on the activity to the class as a whole, highlighting the positive aspects of the learners' performance as well as any areas of their performance that the class as a whole could work on to improve. The teacher then writes

Observation schedule

Name _____

Focus of assessment	Comments
Overall impression	
Accuracy	
Fluency	
Appropriateness	
Intelligibility	
Comprehension	
Strength/s of your spoken English	
Area/s for improvement	

Fig. 22. An observation schedule for assessing spoken genres. (From Paltridge 1998, 179.)

TABLE 6. Criteria for Assessing Spoken Genres

Levels	Overall Impression	Accuracy	Fluency	Appropriacy	Intelligibility	Comprehension
Beginner	Nonuser. Cannot communicate in English at all.					
Elementary	Intermittent user. Communication occurs only sporadically.	Very limited grasp of lexical, grammatical, and discourse patterns.	Utterances consist of isolated words or short, memorized phrases. Frequent pauses may occur. Lack of range, subtlety, and flexibility.	Use of language minimally appropriate to genre, context, and intention.	Can convey only very simple meanings. Concentration and constant verification necessary on the part of the listener. Lacking strategies to compensate for low level of language ability.	Can understand only slow, careful speech. Frequently requires repetition.
Pre-intermediate	Limited user. Neither productive skills nor receptive skills allow continuous communication.	Limited grasp of lexical, grammatical, and discourse patterns. Initial grasp of functional language use.	Speech hesitant, but self-correction occurs. Little ability to take the initiative in developing a conversation. Limited range; no subtlety or flexibility.	Use of language appropriate to context and intention within a limited range of genres.	Can convey basic meanings. Can be understood with effort, but patient understanding necessary. Simple mastery of basic communication strategies.	Can understand speech related to familiar topics phrased simply. Repetition may still be required.
Intermediate	Moderate user. Can get by without serious breakdowns. However, misunderstandings and errors may still occur.	Moderate grasp of lexical, grammatical, and discourse patterns, enabling the expression of a broader range of meanings.	Can sustain conversation, but reformulation sometimes necessary. Moderate range, subtlety, and flexibility.	Use of language generally appropriate to context and intention within a moderate range of genres.	Can be understood without undue difficulty when discussing familiar topics, but problems may arise with detailed explanations. Moderate command of a range of communication strategies.	Can generally understand and interpret meanings related to familiar subjects spoken by a native speaker at normal speed.
Upper Intermediate	Competent user. Copes well in most situations. Will have occasional misunderstandings or errors.	Competent grasp of lexical, grammatical, and discourse patterns, as well as functional language use.	Can generally engage in spontaneous conversation on most general purpose topics. Competent range, subtlety, and flexibility.	Use of language generally appropriate to context and intention within a range of genres.	Communicates meanings competently in general communication contexts. Competent command of a range of communication strategies.	Can understand an extract of information from native speaker speech at normal speed. Some repetition may be required in special-purpose areas.
Advanced	Good user. Copes well in most situations. Can perform competently within own special-purpose areas.	Confident and generally accurate use of lexical, grammatical, and discourse patterns, as well as functional language use.	Can engage in spontaneous conversation on general topics as well as matters relevant to own special-purpose interests. Good range, subtlety, and flexibility.	Use of language mainly appropriate to context and intention within a good range of genres.	Communicates meanings well in general and within own special-purpose genres. Good command of a range of communication strategies.	Can understand and extract information from most native speaker speech. Will also have some competency within own special-purpose areas.

Source: Adapted from Paltridge 1992, 252–53.

up individual assessments of each learner's performance under the categories listed in figure 22. The teacher makes appointments for the students to come and discuss their individual assessments. When discussing their assessments, the teacher asks the students to identify from the assessment one particular area that they will work on for their next in-class observation and assessment. The assessment is repeated after a further period of instruction, using the previous assessment as the starting point for the observation and feedback.

Genre-Based Placement Testing

Paltridge (1992) describes an EAP placement test that incorporates a focus on the relationship between genres in academic settings. Students listen to an academic lecture, read an academic article, then write an academic essay. The test is integrated in terms of content and text type in that the language samples used for the test draw on a common topic (the problems students face studying overseas) and rhetorical patterning (in this case, problem-solution texts). The assessment criteria draw on a set of analytic scales that describe different levels of performance abilities. The criteria used to assess the students' written language proficiency are shown in table 7.

Portfolio Assessment

An assessment approach particularly suited to genre-based teaching is *portfolio assessment*. A portfolio is a collection of pieces of work that a student has produced over a period of time in a particular course of study. Detailed feedback is provided when the work is returned to the student. The assessor provides a provisional grade for each piece of work, as well as details of the criteria employed for the awarding of each grade. The student is then given the opportunity to revise his or her work for an end-of-course portfolio presentation. Depending on the nature of the particular course, this may include all of the student's work or pieces of work selected by the student to represent his or her best performance. The final grade for the student's work is given on the basis of the reworked portfolio presentation.

Portfolio assessment is regularly used in composition classes in the United States. Peter Elbow and Pat Belanoff, in their essay "State University of New York at Stony Brook Portfolio-Based Evaluation Program" (1991), describe the use of portfolio assessment in an undergraduate composition class. Their students' portfolios are made up of

TABLE 7. Criteria for Assessing Written Genres

Levels	Overall Impression	Ideas and Argument	Accuracy	Fluency	Appropriacy	Intelligibility
Beginner	Nonwriter. Cannot write in English at all.					
Elementary	Intermittent writer. Very difficult to follow.	Evidence of few ideas with no apparent development. Little apparent coherence to the text.	Very limited grasp of lexical and grammatical patterns. Little grasp of conventions of punctuation and spelling and use of cohesive devices.	Isolated words or short stock phrases only. Very short text.	Use of language (including layout) minimally appropriate to genre, text type, and communicative goal.	Can convey only very simple meanings. Concentration and constant verification necessary on the part of the reader.
Intermediate	Limited writer. Rather difficult to follow.	Limited range of ideas expressed. Development may be restricted and often incomplete or unclear. Information is not arranged coherently.	Limited grasp of lexical and grammatical patterns and use of cohesive devices. Weaknesses in punctuation and/or spelling.	Texts may be simple, showing little development. Limited range of vocabulary and grammatical and discourse structures.	Use of language generally appropriate to genre, text type, and communicative goal within a limited range of genres and text types. Layout generally appropriate to genre.	Can convey basic meanings, although with some difficulty.
Upper Intermediate	Moderate writer. Fairly easy to read and understand. Texts generally well organized.	Moderate range of ideas expressed. Topic development is present, but may still lack some detail and supporting statements. Information is generally arranged coherently.	Moderate grasp of lexical and grammatical patterns and use of cohesive devises, enabling the expression of a broader range of meanings. Occasional faults in punctuation and spelling.	Texts show increased development. Writes with a fair range and variety of vocabulary and grammatical and discourse structures.	Use of language generally appropriate to genre, text type, and communicative goal within a moderate range of genres and text types. Textual organization and layout generally appropriate to genre and text type.	Broadly able to convey meanings, although errors can interfere with communication.
Advanced	Competent writer. Easy to read from start to finish. Texts generally well organized.	Good range and progression of ideas expressed and coherently arranged, although there may still be isolated problems. Ideas and evidence are relevant, but more detail may still be desirable.	Competent grasp of lexical and grammatical patterns, although problems may still occur with punctuation and spelling.	Can generally write spontaneously on general topics. Competent use of a range of vocabulary and grammatical and discourse structures.	Use of language generally appropriate to genre, text type, and communicative goal within a range of text types. Textual organization and layout appropriate to genre and text type.	Communicates meanings effectively. Only occasional interference due to errors.
Special Purpose	Good writer. Can write well within general and own special-purpose areas. Able to produce organized, coherent, and cohesive discourse.	Good range of relevant ideas are coherently expressed. Evidence is presented and discussed. Where appropriate, a point of view is presented and developed.	Confident and generally accurate use of lexical and grammatical patterns, cohesive devices, punctuation, and spelling.	Writes well on general topics and on matters relevant to own special-purpose interests. Good range of grammatical structures and vocabulary.	Use of language mainly appropriate to genre, text type, and communicative goal within a good range of genres and text types. Textual organization and layout appropriate to genre and text type.	Communicates meanings competently and effectively; qualified intelligibility in certain special-purpose areas. Can generally be understood without any difficulty.

Source: Adapted from Paltridge 1992, 248–49.

one piece of narrative, descriptive, or expressive writing; an academic essay; a piece of writing that analyzes another essay; and one piece of in-class writing. The portfolio is assessed by the class teacher plus one other teacher, both of whom have undergone marker training sessions.

Portfolio assessment is also being increasingly used in university second language writing programs. Ann Johns (1995b) describes an example of the use of portfolio assessment in a writing program for undergraduate ESL students at San Diego State University. The students' portfolios include such pieces of writing as library assignments, out-of-class essays, abstracts, summaries, and in-class examination responses. In *Text, Role, and Context: Developing Academic Literacies* (1997), Johns discusses the use of portfolios further. She discusses three possible portfolio models: reading portfolios, writing portfolios, and portfolios for students taking "linked," or "adjunct," classes, that is, classes linked to studies in the students' subject areas. Figure 23 shows an example of portfolio assessment from an advanced-level EAP course.

In her chapter on portfolio assessment, Ann Johns describes the basic features of portfolios.

- Portfolios should be put together over time.
- Portfolios should normally contain no more than five items (and can, in some cases, be based on one larger piece of work).
- Items in portfolios should reflect the goals of the particular program.
- Portfolios should encourage learners to reflect on their learning.

It is important that students be involved in the selection of work for inclusion in the portfolio, as the ability to recognize the value and quality of one's work is an important aspect of learning. Students should develop new attitudes about their work as a result of portfolios (Felder 1992).

End-of-Course Assessment

At the end of this course you need to present a portfolio of the best work you have produced during the course. You should include only pieces of work you have been given feedback on and have revised on the basis of this feedback.

Your portfolio should include

- A formal letter (e.g., a letter requesting information on a course of study at a college or university)
- A curriculum vitae
- An academic essay
- A summary of a reading or listening text
- An extract from your writing journal

Fig. 23. An example of portfolio assessment

Portfolios can effectively replace end-of-course examinations, as they are fairer for students and give a better view of their learning and of their accomplishments (Johns 1997).They allow a more complex view of complex activities and therefore have a higher level of validity than have single, isolated instances of evaluation (Hamp-Lyons 1991). Portfolio assessment provides an opportunity to draw together objectives and process models of evaluation by focusing on both the process and the product of learning. It also provides a context in which assessment is regarded not merely as a means of measuring results but also, in Geoff Brindley's (1989) terms, "as an aid to learning" (5).

Another strength of portfolio assessment is that it allows students to see that first responses, although valid, need not be final ones. Portfolio assessment makes teachers allies of their students in that they work with their students to help them achieve their best performance possible. It also enables students to demonstrate their potential for future development (Elbow and Belanoff 1991).

Tasks and Discussion Questions

1. Principles of genre-based assessment

Review the summary of principles for genre-based assessment described in this chapter and consider how you would apply these principles in a particular language learning situation.

2. Assessing spoken genres

Consider how you might use the criteria for spoken genres in table 6 in this chapter to assess the speaking skills of a particular group of learners.

3. Assessing written genres

Consider how you might use the criteria for written genres in table 7 in this chapter to assess the writing skills of a particular group of learners.

4. Assessing genre-based instruction

Use the framework for assessing a genre-based teaching and learning cycle in figure 21 in this chapter to plan the evaluation of a lesson or series of genre-based lessons you have planned using this cycle.

5. Portfolio assessment

Read James Dean Brown's chapter on portfolios in his edited volume *New Ways of Classroom Assessment* (1998) and consider how you might use portfolio assessment in a particular language teaching situation.

Further Reading

Brown, J. D., ed. 1998. *New Ways of Classroom Assessment.* Alexandria, VA: TESOL. See pp. 6–33, "Portfolios."

Fulcher, G. 1998. Assessing writing. In G. Fulcher, ed., *Writing in the English Language Classroom.* Hertfordshire, UK: Prentice-Hall Europe ELT.

Johns, A. M. 1997. *Text, Role, and Context: Developing Academic Literacies.* Cambridge: Cambridge University Press. See chapter 8, "Putting Tenets into Practice: Using Portfolios in Literacy Classrooms."

Macken, M., and D. Slade. 1993. Assessment: A foundation for effective learning in the school context. In B. Cope and M. Kalantzis, eds., *The Powers of Literacy: A Genre Approach to Teaching Writing.* London: Falmer.

Paltridge, B. 1992. EAP placement testing: An integrated approach. *English for Specific Purposes* 11 (3): 243–68.

Paltridge, B. 1998. Observation, feedback, and setting individual learning goals. In J. D. Brown, ed., *New Ways of Classroom Assessment.* Alexandria, VA: TESOL.

Chapter 7

Directions for Further Research and Development

Clearly, many issues in the area of applied genre studies require further investigation. One important consideration involves the appropriate units for the analysis of genres (Dudley-Evans 1995c). For example, are linguistic descriptions of genres enough? Dudley-Evans argues, as do Bazerman and others, that solely textual descriptions of genres are not enough. As Bazerman (1988) has argued, "attempts to understand genre by the texts themselves are bound to fail" (7). I agree with this view and have aimed to suggest in this book ways in which nonlinguistic (as well as linguistic) aspects of genres can be explored in the language learning classroom.

Another important question concerns whether genre is in fact a linguistic notion at all. Clearly, this depends on how you define the domain of linguistics. If you take the view that linguistics is concerned with understanding how human beings process and use language, genre most certainly is a linguistic notion. This does not mean, however, that everything that can be said about genres must relate to observable linguistic phenomena. There is as much "outside the text" that is important to consider in the teaching and learning of genres as there is in the text itself. Sigmund Ongstad (personal communication with the author, March 1997) suggests that genre is a "non-observable phenomena" in that we can see the text but cannot (in physical terms) "see the genre." A genre is, in a sense, an abstraction that provides us with a framework for the production and interpretation of language in particular social and cultural contexts (Swales 1993).

Other questions that require further investigation concern the relationship between genre and register, how a genre is identified, and how the boundaries of structural elements can be identified (Hunston 1995). These theoretical questions have important implications for the language learning classroom in that they have an impact on how teachers view and take up the notion of genre in teaching.

A further question concerns the notion of genre-specific language itself. Both systemic and ESP genre studies have, in their own way, examined this notion. Genre-specific language is also given attention in the area of corpus linguistics, that is, the study of language using large databases, or *corpora,* of naturally occurring language (see "Genre and Corpus Studies" in this chapter).

There is clearly a need for more descriptions of the genres that language learners need to control. This is particularly the case with genres that are difficult for learners to observe or to obtain "best examples" of, such as seminar presentations, scholarship applications, and job interviews (Swales 1996). There is also a need for more genre-based studies in the area of English in professional settings and in the many other communicative contexts in which learners find themselves. Recent research has shown that there is often a serious mismatch between how workplace genres are taught and how they are actually used in particular settings (see, e.g., Dias et al. 1999).

There is a great shortage of genre-based descriptions in languages other than English, which could provide the basis for cross-cultural comparisons and for the teaching of genres in these particular languages. There is a need for more "situated" genre studies that go beyond the text and examine the setting in which a genre is located and its particular means of production (see, e.g., Swales 1998; Prior 1998; Dias et al. 1999). We also need a greater understanding of the relationship between genres and accompanying visual representations, earlier examined in the work of Johns (1998), Miller (1998), and Kress and van Leeuwen (1990, 1996).

There are also questions about the relationship between genre and ideology—in particular, how this relationship might be addressed in the language learning classroom. Pennycook (1996) for example, discusses the tension between teaching the "genres of power" and teaching that both acknowledges and fosters diversity (see "Genre and Critical Discourse Analysis" in this chapter).

Genre and Contrastive Rhetoric

When speakers from different countries and cultures interact, more than one set of social and cultural norms and assumptions are at work. Information and argument, for example, are organized differently in different cultures. The meaning behind different speech acts varies. There are also cultural differences in the ways different genres are spoken and written in different languages and cultures. The area of research that examines these sorts of difference is commonly called *contrastive rhetoric.*

Although many studies in this area have focused on academic writing (see, e.g., Connor 1996; Duszak 1997; Taylor and Chen 1991; Lowe 1996), some studies have examined other genres as well. For example, Mauranen (1993) has examined Finnish and English economic reports, looking for language used "to talk about the text" (e.g., text connectors, summary statements, attitude markers, and commentaries). She found significant intercultural variation between the two language groups, with Anglo-American writers using more talk about text than did Finnish writers. This, she argues, is due to a greater concern on the part of Anglo-American writers for guiding their readers through their texts.

Business letters in Japanese, French, and English have been found to be more reader-oriented than English letters, French business letters more writer-oriented, and Japanese letters more oriented toward the "space" between the reader and the writer (Jenkins and Hinds 1987). Differences have also been found in the structural organization of Japanese business letters compared to French and English business letters. Different levels of tone and formality have also been found in between in Japanese, French, and English business letters.

Comparative examinations of the writing of native and nonnative speakers of English have also been carried out. Maier's (1992) study of politeness strategies in business letters found "striking differences in the politeness strategies used by each group [of language users]" (189).

A cross-cultural examination of the introductions section of linguistics articles written in Spanish and English found rhetorical patterns and linguistic features that were different, not due to the language backgrounds of the writers or the languages of the publications, but due to the context of the publications and, in particular, differing relationships between the writers and the discourse community (Burgess 1997).

Cultural expectations and culturally appropriate behavior cannot be described simply in terms of linguistic models (Bloor and Bloor 1995). Teachers need to heighten and refine students' cross-cultural awareness "so that they are able to express themselves as they choose" (Thomas 1983, 91).

Ryuko Kubota (2000) calls for studies of *critical contrastive rhetoric,* that is, studies that examine cultural differences in language and communication and do not essentialize the notion of culture and cultural differences as if they were neutral and permanent truths but rather see them as dynamic and situated in relations of power and ideologies. There is clearly a need for many more studies to be carried out in this particular area, especially now that English is increasingly becoming the language of international business, international conferences, international education, the international communications network, and international travel. Often, in interactions in these areas, English is not the native language of either speaker but is the language most likely to be used to bridge the language gap between speakers. Contrastive studies can help us understand something of the nature of that gap.

Genre and Corpus Studies

Many genre studies have aimed to identify genre-specific language. Some corpus-based studies, however, have suggested that this notion might be more complex than has previously been thought. Biber (1992), for example, argues that different kinds of text are complex in different ways. Biber (1988) has looked at the language features of twenty-three different genres, from such written genres as press reports, novels, and personal and professional letters to such spoken genres as telephone conversations, debates, and speeches. To account for the "complexity of discourse complexity," Biber proposes a framework for text analysis based on an analysis of linguistic features combined with an examination of such dimensions as "abstract versus nonabstract," "narrative versus nonnarrative," and "explicit versus situation-specific reference."

Many genre analysts are equally aware of the complexity of genre-specific language, pointing out that such descriptions need to be "probabilistic" rather than "deterministic" (Halliday 1991; Eggins and Martin 1997); that is, they need to be based on a "more likely/less likely," rather than an "either/or," position of language description. Genre-based descriptions need to describe the range of linguistic features that may typically occur in particular genres, rather than presenting descriptions that assume uniformity among all instances of a particular genre.

Corpus-based studies of genre-specific language have provided useful information for the language learning classroom. Master (1987), for example, used a corpus of fifty thousand words to look at the use of the definite article in scientific articles and found that *the* was used 38 percent of the time, no article 54 percent of the time, and *a* or *an* 8 percent of the time. He also found that *the* occurred in the subject position 71 percent of the time and in the object position only 12 percent of the time. This information is clearly valuable for language learning classrooms.

An examination of a corpus of articles from the journal *Nature* identified the verbs used in descriptions of previous research (Dudley-Evans 1994). The study identified the most common verbs that were used in such descriptions, as well as other verbs that were used less frequently for the same communicative purpose.

Flowerdew (1994b) used a corpus made up of transcriptions of biology lectures and the textbook that was used to accompany the lectures. The lecture data comprised 92,939 words; the textbook material, 90,482 words. He found that the textbook material was much more lexically dense than the lecture material. The textbook also had a wider vocabulary range, longer average word length, and more complex noun phrases than the lectures. He also observed that the lectures made greater use of first and second pronouns, "boosters" (e.g., "actually," "exactly," and "particularly"), "downtoners" (e.g., "a bit," "just," and "only"), modals, and demonstrative pronouns (such as "this" and "that").

Patterns of use that are revealed in corpus studies "often run counter to our expectations based on intuition" (Biber, Conrad, and Reppen 1994, 169). There is, further, often a mismatch between the language presented in published ESL teaching materials and the observations made of language use in corpus-based studies (Ljung 1991; Kennedy 1992). Corpus studies clearly have much to offer descriptions of genres and their application in the language learning classroom, even if, as yet, there is still some uncertainty as to how such vast amounts of linguistic information can be handled in a language learning classroom (Swales 2000a). (See Simpson and Swales 2001 for recent work in the area of corpus linguistics in North America; also Bondi 1999 for a corpus-based examination of genres in the field of economics.)

Genre and Critical Discourse Analysis

Attention is not always given to the ideological dimensions of genre in language learning classrooms (Hyon 1996). Sarah Benesch (1993) argues that all forms of ESL instruction are ideological, whether we are conscious of it or not. Diane Belcher and George Braine (1995) make a similar argument, pointing out that academic literacy is neither neutral nor value free. As Benesch argues, teachers can, through instructional choices, encourage students to think critically about their education and the world or discourage them from doing this.

In a discussion of the teaching of EAP, Benesch (1993) argues:

> the good intentions and hard work of EAP researchers may make life harder for both ESL faculty and students because of EAP's accommodation to traditional academic practices which limit the participation of nonnative-speaking students in academic culture. (713)

Benesch suggests that an alternative to accepting this "ideology of accommodation" is to take on an "ideology of resistance" and a pedagogy of critical academic ESL that gives students "opportunities to discover and critically examine the conventions of the academic discourse community" (Clark 1992, 137) and the amount of negotiation that is possible in terms of the ways in which their academic performance will be assessed. For example, do students have to write exams, or can they write essays instead, and if writing essays is not enough, why not (Benesch 1999, 2001)? It is important, then, to consider the place of a critical approach to genre-based language teaching, including the types and levels of classrooms in which such an approach might most usefully be introduced (Hyon 1996).

A critical perspective on genre might explore the connections between discourse, language learning, language use, and the social and political contexts in which these occur. It needs to do this in a way that deals critically with the norms and expectations of particular discourse communities and raises issues of social, economic, and political concern but, nevertheless, provides students with the tools they need to succeed (Pennycook 1997). It also needs to provide a context in which students are able to reflect on their own experiences as they relate to values of particular discourse communities (Kanpol 1990).

Genre is not an ideology-free, objective process that can be "separated from the social realities and processes which it contributes to maintaining" (Threadgold 1989, 103). Genres are not just linguistic categories; they are "among the very processes by which dominant ideologies are reproduced, transmitted, and potentially changed" (Threadgold 1989, 107). Performing a genre is never just the reformulation of a linguistic model but always the performance of a politically and historically significant process. The teaching of genres should, according to Threadgold, aim to "make visible" the social construction and transmission of ideologies, power relationships, and social identities.

A critical perspective on genre might explore such issues as gender, ethnicity, cultural difference, ideology, and identity and how these are reflected in particular texts (Pennycook 1997). It might also explore how these relations can be drawn to learners' attention so that they are aware of how they are positioned by particular texts. Dealing with these questions in a language learning classroom clearly requires a reasonable level of language proficiency. These questions can, however, be dealt with selectively to help learners better understand what a text might assume of them and how they can present a particular position, should they wish to do so.

A critical perspective on genre goes beyond description and explanation to "deconstructing" and "challenging" texts. This emphasis might include tracing underlying ideologies from the linguistic features of a text, unpacking particular biases and ideological presuppositions, and relating the text to other texts and to the readers' own experiences and beliefs (Clark 1995). This is one further direction in which future work could be profitably directed.

Limitations of Genre-Based Instruction

It is important to consider the possible limitations of genre-based language teaching. One limitation might involve the notion of genre itself; that is, how do we identify a spoken or written text as an instance of particular genre? What are its characteristic features? Can these be described in linguistic terms alone, or does their description require a broader set of categories? One argument that has been made is that genre knowledge not only entails textual knowledge but also includes social and cultural knowledge. Exactly what this knowledge is can, however, be difficult to identify, especially if teachers are teaching a genre that they themselves do not regularly use or, indeed, have never used.

The issue of teacher knowledge becomes more complex when teachers are not native speakers of the language they are teaching and when they are teaching in a community in which the target language is not spoken. There is also the problem of gaining access to authentic examples of spoken and written genres, especially if the teaching situation is a foreign language classroom (i.e., outside of the country where the target language is the language most used). There is also the difficulty of employing a genre-based approach in multigoal classrooms, that is, classrooms where there are no common goals among learners. Here, it might be more useful to focus on more everyday genres (e.g., casual conversation and the kinds of genre people use in everyday spoken interactions) than on some of the more specific-purpose genres that tend to be focused on in much genre-based instruction.

John Swales (2000b) summarizes further concerns that have been expressed in relation to genre-based teaching. The first of these is the question of "repression versus expression"; that is, does a genre-based approach limit student expression through its use of model texts and its focus on audience expectations? This need not necessarily be the case but is clearly something teachers need to keep in mind when focusing on genres in their classrooms. Teachers equally need to help students bring their own individual voices into their work within the context of recurring genre patterns. Learners need to see to what extent they might or might not need to imitate certain genre patterns and on what occasions they might resist these patterns. Equally, students need to understand to what extent and on what occasions they can "border-cross" in their use of particular genres. In some areas of communication, this may not be so easily possible, but in others, it may be quite acceptable.

The "rules" of these "games," as with genres themselves, are constantly changing. The E-mail message is an example of a genre that has changed many rules, conventions, and expectations for genre-specific communications. The genre of the university lecture is changing, especially with the introduction of new technologies into teaching and learning in the field of higher education (see, e.g., Myers 2000). Academic writing within some disciplines is also changing, especially with the influence of what has been termed the "postmodern turn" in the "new humanities" and social sciences (Hodge 1998).

One genre may be embedded in another. For example, a letter, a story, or a newspaper article may be used for another "conventionally distinct" genre, such as an advertisement to sell a product or a job advertisement (Bhatia 1995b, 1997). Equally, genre mixing may occur—for example, when a book review describes and evaluates a book and also promotes it.

Heather Kay and Tony Dudley-Evans (1998) asked a group of language teachers what they thought of the notion of genre and what concerns they might have about using it in the classroom. The teachers were from a number of different countries and included native and nonnative speakers of English. One concern the teachers had was the danger that a genre-based approach might become too prescriptive. They pointed out the need for teachers to highlight the variation that occurs in particular genres and to consider why this might be. They stressed the importance of contextualizing genres in the classroom by discussing their purpose, audience, and underlying beliefs and values before discussing their language features. The teachers said learners should be exposed to a wide variety of sample texts within a particular genre and that these should be both authentic and suitable for their learners. They thought that a genre-based approach should be used in combination with other approaches, such as process approaches (in the case of writing) and communicative approaches (in the case of speaking).

The teachers in Kay and Dudley-Evans's group said, however, that they considered a genre-based approach especially suitable for beginner and intermediate students, as it enables them "to produce a text that serves its intended purpose" (Kay and Dudley-Evans 1998, 310). They found model texts especially useful at this level, as they gave learners confidence and "something to fall back on." They concluded that genre provides a useful framework for the language learning classroom, as long as it is made clear to learners that the genres are just possible models and not set patterns of form.

There is often a tension between process approaches to teaching writing, where individual expression is encouraged, and product- and genre-oriented approaches, which focus more on the expectations of the audience and discourse community. Each of these approaches, however, is complementary to the other (Badger and White 2000). The weakness of purely product-oriented approaches is the limited attention sometimes given to process skills, such as planning, drafting, and reworking texts. A key strength of a genre approach is its focus on social context and communicative purpose. These perspectives can be usefully drawn together. Effective communication involves knowledge about language (as in product and genre approaches), knowledge about social context and purpose (as in a genre approach), and skills in using language (as in a process approach). Teachers need to focus on each of these aspects of generic competence (see Bhatia 2000) to help learners produce texts that respond to both the how and the what of particular communicative situations.

Mary Shih (1999) discusses the issue of teaching in a foreign language classroom where authentic language samples may be difficult to obtain, where the teacher's knowledge of authentic language use might be limited, and where it might be hard for students to find a real-life audience for their English-language communications. She suggests looking for authentic English-language texts in local bookstores, newsstands, and tourist offices. Useful texts she has found in these kinds of location include local English-language periodicals, international English-language newspapers and magazines, and brochures and maps aimed at English-speaking tourists. She also suggests that teachers in these situations enlist the help of foreign teachers, who may know better than their students where suitable authentic English-language texts might be found. Shih also suggests making using of the Internet for authentic written texts and encouraging students to join electronic discussion lists and chat rooms. Another possibility is to get individual students or groups of students, with the help of their teacher, to set up E-mail communications with native speaker students overseas, so that the students might exchange information about each other's countries while simultaneously gaining real-life communicative practice. Students can also be encouraged to correspond with people in an English-speaking country or in countries where English is a lingua franca of communication. Shih had students in her U.S. culture class at Central Normal University in China write to individuals and organizations in the United States for information on cross-cultural topics they were studying and then use this information for preparing and writing group research papers. As she points out, EFL students are not always motivated to communicate in English if they feel there is little chance they might really interact with foreigners. Communicating through English, she suggests, does not necessarily require face-to-face contact with native speakers. There are many ways in which students can use English to obtain information and gain other perspectives, and there are an increasing number of ways in which EFL students can conduct electronically mediated communications with native speakers of English abroad.

An example of how genre-based instruction can be usefully employed for low-level learners is provided by Jenny Green (1992). Using a genre-based teaching and learning cycle (see my chap. 2 in the present book), she takes a group of immigrant learners with low levels of English language proficiency and literacy through the genres they need to command to visit a local health center. With extensive preparatory work on setting the context and with specifically focused language work, she prepares them to make an appointment at the health center. This preparation includes a focus on the appointment card, the appointment book, client registration forms, and telephoning to make an appointment. She carefully highlights the culture-specific nature of each of these genres and the role they play in helping the learners achieve their goal, that is, making an appointment to see a doctor. She models the various genres for her learners and moves back and forth through the stages of the teaching and learning cycle in response to the needs of her group of learners. She also highlights the significance and purpose of each of the genres as she progresses through her series of lessons. By choosing genres that are important for her group of learners and taking them carefully through each of the stages of her instruction, she provides a setting in which her learners come to understand and use the particular genres in their own, independent ways.

An example of genre-based teaching with lower-level learners in a foreign language setting—computer science students writing in English at a Japanese university—is provided by Laurence Anthony (2000). Anthony argues strongly for the explicit teaching of the language and discourse features of the genres his students need to control. To avoid the dangers of overgeneralization of language rules, he bases his teaching materials on a large-scale sample of real-life texts from the students' area of study. He also provides his students with examples of the same genre in other study areas, to show how the same genre can vary across disciplines. Students carry out their own genre analyses of sample texts, independent of the teacher, and bring their results back to the classroom. Where further variation is found, it is incorporated into the genre model being developed in the classroom. Anthony acknowledges that it can be difficult to explain nonformal aspects of the texts, such as writer purpose and audience, to students at lower levels of language proficiency. He deals with this difficulty by drawing on the learners' experience of the genre in their own language and culture and comparing this with the genre under study. As he points out, the context of a foreign language classroom can be very different from many second language (and native speaker) settings where genre-based teaching has been employed. As a result, it often needs particular explicit teaching strategies that account for what the learners already know, as well as what they need to know.

This chapter has suggested many areas in which further research in the area of applied genre studies could be usefully directed. Teachers need to understand better the impact of genre-based instruction on the teaching and learning of spoken and written genres. Teachers need to better understand the nature of genre-specific language if they are to helpfully focus on this in the language learning classroom. Teachers also need to better understand the settings of particular genres and how teachers can unpack complex social relations, expectations, and assumptions in ways that are useful to learners.

Clearly, much research and development still needs to be carried out in relation to genre-based language teaching and learning. However, much that has already been done in ESP, systemic, and new rhetoric genre studies is of enormous value for language learning classrooms. The aim of this book has been to give an insight into some of this work and to suggest ways in which what we have seen so far can be taken up in the language learning classroom.

Tasks and Discussion Questions

1. Genre and corpus studies

See Tribble's (1996, 148–50) suggestion for a task in which learners carry out their own corpus-based investigations into genre-specific language. Plan a task for a group of learners, focusing on a genre that they need to be able to use and on an aspect of language that would be useful to examine.

2. Genre and ideology

Read Benesch 1993, Canagarajah 1993, and Cope and Kalantzis 1993 and summarize what their authors say about genre and ideology. Do you agree with their views? What are some of the implications of their views for the language learning classroom?

3. Genre and critical discourse analysis

Choose a text that you think would be useful to focus on in a language learning classroom. Carry out an analysis of it in terms of the knowledge, assumptions, and point of view assumed by the text. Consider how the context and purpose of the text impacts both what is said and how it is said. How is the relationship between the author and the intended audience of the text expressed through language choices, and how does this position potential readers of the text? How do language features (e.g., the use of attitudinal verbs, adjectives, adverbs, and modals expressing permission or obligation) contribute to the expression of a particular worldview? Based on Gollin 1992 and Clark 1995, consider how you might use this kind of analysis in a language learning classroom.

Further Reading

Anthony, L. 2000. Implementing genre analysis in a foreign language classroom. *TESOL Matters* 10 (4): 18.

Badger, R., and G. White. 2000. A process genre approach to teaching writing. *ELT Journal* 54 (2): 153–60.

Benesch, S. 1993. ESL, ideology, and the politics of pragmatism. *TESOL Quarterly* 27 (4): 705–17.

Biber, D., S. Conrad, and R. Reppen. 1994. Corpus-based approaches to issues in applied linguistics. *Applied Linguistics* 15 (2): 169–89.

Canagarajah, A. S. 1993. Critical ethnography of a Sri Lankan classroom: Ambiguities in student opposition to reproduction through ESL. *TESOL Quarterly* 27 (4): 601–26.

Comber, B. 1994. Critical literacy: An introduction to Australian debates and perspectives. *Journal of Curriculum Studies* 26 (6): 655–68.

Connor, U. 1996. *Contrastive Rhetoric: Cross-Cultural Aspects of Second Language Writing.* Cambridge: Cambridge University Press.

Cope, B., and M. Kalantzis. 1993. Introduction: How a genre approach to literacy can transform the way writing is taught. In B. Cope and M. Kalantzis, eds., *The Powers of Literacy: A Genre Approach to Teaching Writing.* London: Falmer.

Hammond, J., and M. Macken-Horarick. 1999. Critical literacy: Challenges and questions for ESL classrooms. *TESOL Quarterly* 33 (3): 528–44.

Kay, H., and T. Dudley-Evans. 1998. Genre: What teachers think. *ELT Journal* 52 (4): 308–14.

Pennycook, A. 1997. Critical applied linguistics and education. In R. Wodak and D. Corson, eds., *Encyclopedia of Language and Education,* vol. 1. Dordrecht: Kluwer.

Shih, M. 1999. More than practicing language: Communicative reading and writing for Asian settings. *TESOL Journal* 8 (4): 20–25.

Bibliography

Adamson, H. D. 1990. ESL students' use of academic skills in content courses. *English for Specific Purposes* 9 (1): 67–87.

Allison, D. 1999. Key concepts in ELT: Genre. *ELT Journal* 53 (2): 144.

Anthony, L. 2000. Implementing genre analysis in a foreign language classroom. *TESOL Matters* 10 (3): 18.

Atkinson, D. 1996. Genre analysis in ESP: Some central issues. *TESOL Matters* 6 (2): 11.

Badger, R., and G. White. 2000. A process genre approach to teaching writing. *ELT Journal* 54 (2): 153–60.

Batstone, R. 1994. *Grammar*. Oxford: Oxford University Press.

Bazerman, C. 1988. *Shaping Written Knowledge*. Madison: University of Wisconsin Press.

Bazerman, C. 1994. Systems of genres and the enactment of social intentions. In A. Freedman and P. Medway, eds., *Genre and the New Rhetoric*. London: Taylor and Francis.

Belcher, D., and G. Braine, eds. 1995. *Academic Writing in a Second Language: Essays on Research and Pedagogy*. Norwood, NJ: Ablex.

Benesch, S. 1993. ESL, ideology, and the politics of pragmatism. *TESOL Quarterly* 27 (4): 705–17.

Benesch, S. 1999. Rights analysis: Studying power relations in an academic setting. *English for Specific Purposes* 18 (4): 313–27.

Benesch, S. 2001. *Critical English for Academic Purposes: Theory, Politics, and Practice*. Mahwah, NJ: Lawrence Erlbaum.

Berkenkotter, C., and T. N. Huckin. 1995. *Genre Knowledge in Disciplinary Communication: Cognition/Culture/Power*. Hillsdale, NJ: Lawrence Erlbaum.

Bhatia, V. K. 1993. *Analysing Genre: Language Use in Professional Settings.* London: Longman

Bhatia, V. K. 1995a. Recent developments in genre theory: Problems and perspectives. In S. Gill, ed., *Proceedings of the International English Language Education Conference: National and International Challenges and Responses.* Kuala Lumpur: Universiti Kebangsaan Malaysia.

Bhatia, V. K. 1995b. Genre-mixing in professional communication: The case of "private intentions" v. "socially recognized purposes." In P. Bruthiaux, T. Boswood, and B. Du-Babcock, eds., *Explorations in English for Professional Communication.* Hong Kong: Department of English, City University of Hong Kong.

Bhatia, V. K. 1997. Genre-mixing in academic introductions. *English for Specific Purposes* 16 (3): 181–95.

Bhatia, V. K. 1999a. Integrating products, processes, purposes, and participants in professional writing. In C. N. Candlin and K. Hyland, eds., *Writing: Texts, Processes, and Practices.* London: Longman.

Bhatia, V. K. 1999b. Analyzing genre: An applied linguistic perspective. Keynote presentation at the Twelfth World Congress of Applied Linguistics, Tokyo, August.

Bhatia, V. K. 2000. Integrating discursive competence and professional practice: A new challenge for ESP. Paper presented at the TESOL colloquium "Rethinking ESP for the New Century," Vancouver, March.

Biber, D. 1988. *Variation across Speech and Writing.* Cambridge: Cambridge University Press.

Biber, D. 1989. A typology of English texts. *Linguistics* 27:3–43.

Biber, D. 1992. On the complexity of discourse complexity: A multidimensional analysis. *Discourse Processes* 15:133–63.

Biber, D., S. Conrad, and R. Reppen. 1994. Corpus-based approaches to issues in applied linguistics. *Applied Linguistics* 15 (2): 169–89.

Bizzell, P. 1982. College composition: Initiation into the academic discourse community. *Curriculum Inquiry* 12:191–207. Reprinted in P. Bizzell, *Academic Discourse and Critical Consciousness* (Pittsburgh: University of Pittsburgh Press, 1992).

Bizzell, P. 1992. *Academic Discourse and Critical Consciousness.* Pittsburgh: University of Pittsburgh Press.

Bloor, M. 1998. English for specific purposes: The preservation of the species. *English for Specific Purposes* 17 (1): 47–66.

Bloor, T., and M. Bloor. 1995. *The Functional Analysis of English: A Hallidayan Approach.* London: Arnold.

Bondi, M. 1999. *English across Genres: Language Variation in the Discourse of Economics.* Modena: Edizioni il Fiorino.

Brindley, G. 1989. Editorial. *Prospect* 4 (3): 5–8.

Brookes, A., and P. Grundy. 1990. *Writing for Study Purposes: A Teacher's Guide to Developing Individual Writing Skills.* Cambridge: Cambridge University Press.

Brookes, A., and P. Grundy, eds. 1988. *Individualisation and Autonomy in Language Learning.* ELT Documents, no. 131. London: Macmillan and Modern English Teacher.

Brown, J. D., ed. 1998. *New Ways of Classroom Assessment.* Alexandria, VA: TESOL.

Bruner, J. S. 1975. The ontogenesis of speech acts. *Journal of Child Language* 2:1–19.

Burgess, S. 1997. Discourse variation across cultures: A genre-analytic study of writing on linguistics. Ph.D. diss., University of Reading.

Burns, A., and H. Joyce. 1997. *Focus on Speaking.* Sydney: National Centre for English Language Teaching and Research, Macquarie University.

Burns, A., H. Joyce, and S. Gollin. 1996. *I See What You Mean: Using Spoken Discourse in the Classroom.* Sydney: National Centre for English Language Teaching and Research, Macquarie University.

Butt, D., R. Fahey, S. Spinks, and C. Yallop. 1995. *Using Functional Grammar.* Sydney: National Centre for English Language Teaching and Research, Macquarie University.

Bygate, M. 1987. *Speaking.* Oxford: Oxford University Press.

Callaghan, M., P. Knapp, and G. Noble. 1993. Genres in practice. In B. Cope and M. Kalantzis, eds., *The Powers of Literacy: A Genre Approach to Teaching Writing.* London: Falmer.

Canagarajah, A. S. 1993. Critical ethnography of a Sri Lankan classroom: Ambiguities in student opposition to reproduction through ESL. *TESOL Quarterly* 27 (4): 601–26.

Carter, R., and M. McCarthy. 1997. *Exploring Spoken English.* Cambridge: Cambridge University Press.

Casanave, C. 1995. Local interactions: Constructing contexts for composing in a graduate sociology program. In D. Belcher and G. Braine, eds., *Academic*

Writing in a Second Language: Essays on Research and Pedagogy. Norwood, NJ: Ablex.

Cazden, C. B. 1988. *Classroom Discourse: The Language of Teaching and Learning.* Portsmouth, NH: Heinemann.

Celce-Murcia, M. 1990. Discourse analysis and grammar instruction. *Annual Review of Applied Linguistics* 11:135–51.

Celce-Murcia, M. 1996. Teaching grammar through discourse: Toward a more future perfect pedagogy. Paper presented at the Fifth National Conference on Community Languages and English for Speakers of Other Languages, Hamilton, New Zealand, September.

Celce-Murcia, M., and E. Olshtain. 2000. *Discourse and context in language teaching: A guide for language teachers.* Cambridge: Cambridge University Press.

Christie, F. 1989. *Language Education.* Oxford: Oxford University Press.

Christie, F. 1996. The role of functional grammar in development of a critical literacy. In G. Bull and M. Anstey, eds., *The Literacy Lexicon.* Sydney: Prentice-Hall.

Christie, F. 1999. Genre theory and ESL teaching: A systemic functional perspective. *TESOL Quarterly* 33 (4): 759–63.

Clark, R. J. 1992. Principles and practice of CLA in the classroom. In N. Fairclough, ed., *Critical Language Awareness.* London: Longman.

Clark, R. J. 1995. Developing critical reading practices. *Prospect* 10 (2): 65–80.

Coe, R. 1994. An arousing and fulfillment of desires: The rhetoric of genre in the process era—and beyond. In A. Freedman and P. Medway, eds., *Genre and the New Rhetoric.* London: Taylor and Francis.

Colman, J., and J. Schiffmann. 1993. *Teaching ESL Literacy to Adults.* Armidale, New South Wales: Language Training Centre, University of New England.

Comber, B. 1994. Critical literacy: An introduction to Australian debates and perspectives. *Journal of Curriculum Studies* 26 (6): 655–68.

Connor, U. 1996. *Contrastive Rhetoric: Cross-Cultural Aspects of Second Language Writing.* Cambridge: Cambridge University Press.

Conway, D., and C. Thaine. 1997. Language awareness issues on a CELTA course from a discourse perspective. Paper presented at the Cambridge Integrated Language Teaching Schemes Conference, Christchurch, New Zealand, August.

Cook, G. 1989. *Discourse.* Oxford: Oxford University Press.

Cope, B., and M. Kalantzis. 1993. Introduction: How a genre approach to literacy can transform the way writing is taught. In B. Cope and M. Kalantzis, eds., *The Powers of Literacy: A Genre Approach to Teaching Writing.* London: Falmer.

Cornish, S. 1992. *Community Access: Curriculum Guidelines.* Sydney: New South Wales Adult Migrant Education Service.

Cox, L. 1998. A genre to remember. In P. Master and D. Brinton, eds., *New Ways in English for Specific Purposes.* Alexandria, VA: TESOL.

Davies, F. 1988. Designing a writing syllabus in English for academic purposes: Process and product. In P. Robinson, ed., *Academic Writing: Process and Product.* ELT Documents, no. 129. London: Macmillan and Modern English Teacher.

Delpit, L. 1998. The politics of teaching literate discourse. In V. Zamel and R. Spack, eds., *Negotiating Academic Literacies.* Mahwah, NJ: Lawrence Erlbaum.

Derewianka, B. 1991. *Exploring How Texts Work.* Rev. ed. Sydney: Primary English Teaching Association.

Dias, P., A. Freedman, P. Medway, and A. Pare. 1999. *Worlds Apart: Acting and Writing in Academic and Workplace Contexts.* Mahwah, NJ: Lawrence Erlbaum.

Donato, R. 2000. Sociocultural contributions to understanding the foreign and second language classroom. In J. P. Lantolf, ed., *Sociocultural Theory and Second Language Learning.* Oxford: Oxford University Press.

Dudley-Evans, T. 1985. *Writing Laboratory Reports.* Melbourne: Thomas Nelson.

Dudley-Evans, T. 1986. Genre analysis: An investigation of the introduction and discussion sections of MSc dissertations. In M. Coulthard, ed., *Talking about Text.* Discourse Analysis Monographs, no. 13. Birmingham, UK: English Language Research, University of Birmingham.

Dudley-Evans, T. 1989. An outline of the value of genre analysis in LSP work. In C. Lauren and M. Nordman, eds., *Special Language: From Humans Thinking to Thinking Machines.* Clevedon: Multilingual Matters.

Dudley-Evans, T. 1993. Variation in communication patterns between discourse communities: The case of highway engineering and plant biology. In G. Blue, ed., *Language, Learning, and Success: Studying through English.* London: Macmillan and Modern English Publications.

Dudley-Evans, T. 1994. Research in English for Specific Purposes. In R. Khoo, ed., *LSP—Problems and Prospects.* Anthology Series, no. 13. Singapore: SEAMEO Regional Language Centre.

Dudley-Evans, T. 1995a. Genre models for the teaching of academic writing to second language speakers: Advantages and disadvantages. *Journal of TESOL France* 2 (2): 181–92. Reprinted in T. Miller, ed., *Functional Approaches to Written Text: Classroom Applications* (Washington, DC: United States Information Agency, 1997).

Dudley-Evans, T. 1995b. Common core and specific approaches to the teaching of academic writing. In D. Belcher and G. Braine, eds., *Academic Writing in a Second Language: Essays on Research and Pedagogy.* Norwood, NJ: Ablex.

Dudley-Evans, T. 1995c. What's the use of genre: Is there more to life than moves? Paper presented at the BAAL/CUP workshop/seminar on genre, Sheffield University, July.

Dudley-Evans, T., and M. J. St. John. 1998. *Developments in English for Special Purposes.* Cambridge: Cambridge University Press.

Duszak, A., ed. 1997. *Culture and Styles of Academic Discourse.* Berlin and New York: Mouton de Gruyter.

Eggins, S., and J. R. Martin. 1997. Genres and registers of discourse. In T. A. Van Dijk, ed., *Discourse as Structure and Process.* London: Sage.

Eggins, S., and D. Slade. 1997. *Analysing Casual Conversation.* London: Cassell.

Elbow, P., and P. Belanoff. 1991. State University of New York at Stony Brook portfolio-based evaluation program. In P. Belanoff and M. Dickson, eds., *Portfolio Grading: Process and Product.* Portsmouth, NH: Boynton/Cook.

Ellis, R. 1992. *Grammar teaching—practice or consciousness raising? Second Language Acquisition and Language Pedagogy.* Clevedon: Multilingual Matters.

Ellis, R. 1993. Talking shop: Second language acquisition research—How does it help teachers? *ELT Journal* 47 (1): 3–11.

Er, E. 1993. Text analysis and diagnostic assessment. *Prospect* 8 (3): 63–77.

Fairclough, N. 1989. *Language and Power.* London: Longman.

Fairclough, N. 1992. Introduction to N. Fairclough, ed., *Critical Language Awareness.* London: Longman.

Fairclough, N. 1993. Critical discourse analysis and the marketization of public discourse: The universities. *Discourse and Society* 4 (2): 133–68.

Feez, S. 1998. *Test-Based Syllabus Design.* Sydney: National Centre for English Language Teaching and Research, Macquarie University.

Felder, R. 1992. Portfolios in high school. 28 October. E-mail circulated to TESOL list (28 October 1992).

Flowerdew, J. 1993. An educational, or process, approach to the teaching of professional genres. *ELT Journal* 47 (4): 305–16.

Flowerdew, J. 1994a. Research of relevance to second language lecture comprehension—an overview. In J. Flowerdew, ed., *Academic Listening: Research Perspectives.* Cambridge: Cambridge University Press.

Flowerdew, J. 1994b. Specific language for specific purposes: Concordancing for the ESP syllabus. In R. Khoo, ed., *LSP—Problems and Prospects.* Anthology Series, no. 13. Singapore: SEAMEO Regional Language Centre.

Flowerdew, L. 2000. Using a genre-based framework to teach organizational structure in academic writing. *ELT Journal* 54 (4): 369–78.

Flowerdew, J., and L. Miller. 1996. Lectures in a second language: Notes towards a cultural grammar. *English for Specific Purposes* 15 (2): 121–40.

Freedman, A. 1999. Beyond the text: Towards understanding the teaching and learning of genres. *TESOL Quarterly* 33 (4): 764–68.

Freedman, A., and P. Medway, eds. 1994. *Genre and the New Rhetoric.* London: Taylor and Francis.

Fulcher, G. 1998. Assessing writing. In G. Fulcher, ed., *Writing in the English Language Classroom.* Hertfordshire, UK: Prentice-Hall Europe ELT.

Gardner, R. 1995. Conversation analysis: Some thought on its applicability to applied linguistics. *Australian Review of Applied Linguistics,* ser. s, 11:97–119.

Gee, S. 1997. Teaching writing: A genre-based approach. In G. Fulcher, ed., *Writing in the English Language Classroom.* Hertfordshire, UK: Prentice-Hall Europe ELT.

Gerot, L., and P. Wignell. 1994. *Making Sense of Functional Grammar.* Gold Coast, Queensland: AEE Publishers.

Gollin, S. 1992. Towards critical literacy in EAP. *Building on Strength.* Vol 2. Sydney: ATESOL.

Grabe, W., and R. Kaplan. 1996. *Theory and Practice of Writing: An Applied Linguistic Perspective.* London: Longman.

Green, J. 1992. *Making the Links.* Melbourne: Adult Migrant Education Services. Video and Workshop Guide.

Guenthner, S., and H. Knoblauch. 1995. Culturally patterned speaking practices—the analysis of communicative genres. *Pragmatics* 5 (1): 1–32.

Hadfield, J. 1984. *Elementary Communication Games.* Surry: Thomas Nelson.

Hadfield, J. 1987. *Advanced Communication Games.* Surry: Thomas Nelson.

Hadfield, J. 1990. *Intermediate Communication Games.* Surry: Thomas Nelson.

Hagan, P., S. Hood, E. Jackson, M. Jones, H. Joyce, and M. Manidis. 1993. *Certificate in Spoken and Written English.* 2d ed. Sydney: New South Wales Adult Migrant Education Service and National Centre for English Language Teaching and Research, Macquarie University.

Halliday, M. A. K. 1989. *Spoken and Written Language.* Oxford: Oxford University Press.

Halliday, M. A. K. 1991. Towards probabilistic interpretations. In E. Ventola, ed., *Functional and Systemic Linguistics: Approaches and Uses.* Berlin: Mouton de Gruyter.

Halliday, M. A. K. 1994. *An Introduction to Functional Grammar.* 2d ed. London: Edward Arnold.

Hammond, J. 1987. An overview of the genre-based approach to the teaching of writing in Australia. *Australian Review of Applied Linguistics* 10 (2): 163–81.

Hammond, J., A. Burns, H. Joyce, D. Brosnan, and L. Gerot. 1992. *English for Social Purposes: A Handbook for Teachers of Adult Literacy.* Sydney: National Centre for English Language Teaching and Research, Macquarie University.

Hammond, J., and M. Mackin-Horarick. 1999. Critical literacy: Challenges and questions for ESL classrooms. *TESOL Quarterly* 33 (3): 528–44.

Hamp-Lyons, L. 1991. Scoring procedures for ESL contexts. In L. Hamp-Lyons, ed., *Assessing Second Language Writing in Academic Contexts.* Norwood, NJ: Ablex.

Harmer, J. 1987. *Teaching and Learning Grammar.* London: Longman.

Harmer, J. 1998. *How to Teach English.* London: Longman.

Hasan, R. 1989a. The structure of a text. In M. A. K. Halliday and R. Hasan, *Language, Context, and Text: Aspects of Language in a Social-Semiotic Perspective.* Oxford: Oxford University Press.

Hasan, R. 1989b. The identity of a text. In M. A. K. Halliday and R. Hasan, *Language, Context, and Text: Aspects of Language in a Social-Semiotic Perspective.* Oxford: Oxford University Press.

Hatch, E. 1986. The experience model of language learning. In R. R. Day, ed., *Talking to Learn: Conversation in Second Language Acquisition.* Rowley, MA: Newbury House.

Hawkins, B. 1988. Scaffolded classroom interaction and its relation to second language acquisition for language minority children. Ph.D. diss., University of California, Los Angeles.

Hedge, T. 1988. *Writing.* Oxford: Oxford University Press.

Hedge, T. 2000. *Teaching and Learning in the Language Classroom.* Oxford: Oxford University Press.

Helgesen, M., S. Brown, and D. Smith. 1996. *Active Listening: Expanding Understanding through Content, Student's Book 3.* Cambridge: Cambridge University Press.

Henry, A., and R. L. Roseberry. 1998. An evaluation of a genre-based approach to the teaching of EAP/ESP writing. *TESOL Quarterly* 32 (1): 147–56.

Hewings, M., and W. Henderson. 1987. A link between genre and schemata: A case study of economics text. *University of Birmingham English Language Research Journal* 7 (1): 156–75.

Hodge, B. 1998. Monstrous knowledge: Doing PhDs in the "new humanities." In A. Lee and B. Green, eds., *Postgraduate studies: Postgraduate pedagogy.* Sydney: Centre for Language and Literacy, Faculty of Education, University of Technology, Sydney.

Holmes, J., and D. Brown. 1976. Developing sociolinguistic competence in a second language. *TESOL Quarterly* 10 (4): 427–29.

Holmes, J., and D. Brown. 1987. Teachers and students learning about compliments. *TESOL Quarterly* 21 (3): 523–46.

Hood, S., and H. Joyce. 1995. Reading in the adult ESL curriculum and classroom. *Prospect* 10 (2): 52–64.

Hood, S., N. Solomon, and A. Burns. 1995. *Focus on Reading.* New ed. Sydney: National Centre for English Language Teaching and Research, Marquarie University.

Hopkins, A., and T. Dudley-Evans. 1988. A genre-based investigation of the discussion section in articles and dissertations. *English for Specific Purposes* 7 (2): 113–22.

Horvarth, B., and S. Eggins. 1995. Opinion texts in conversation. In P. Fries and M. Gregory, eds., *Discourse in Society: Systemic Functional Perspectives.* Norwood, NJ: Ablex.

Huckin, T. 1997. Cultural aspects of genre knowledge. *AILA Review* 12:68–78.

Humphrey, S. 1990. Teaching grammar through genre. *EA Journal* 8 (1): 26–29.

Hunston, S. 1995. Some problems in the study of genre. Paper presented at the BAAL/CUP workshop/seminar on genre, Sheffield University, July.

Hutchinson, T., and A. Waters. 1987. *English for Specific Purposes: A Learning-Centred Approach.* Cambridge: Cambridge University Press.

Hyland, K. 1990. A genre description of the argumentative essay. *RELC Journal* 21 (1): 66–78.

Hyon, S. 1995. A genre-based approach to ESL reading: Implications for North America and Australia. Ph.D. diss., University of Michigan, Ann Arbor.

Hyon, S. 1996. Genre in three traditions: Implications for ESL. *TESOL Quarterly* 30 (4): 693–722.

Jenkins, S., and J. Hinds. 1987. Business letter writing: English, French, and Japanese. *TESOL Quarterly* 21 (2): 327–54.

Johns, A. M. 1988. The discourse communities dilemma: Identifying transferable skills for the academic milieu. *English for Specific Purposes* 7 (1): 55–59.

Johns, A. M. 1990. Coherence as a cultural phenomenon: Employing ethnographic principles in the academic milieu. In U. Connor and A. M. Johns, eds., *Coherence in Writing.* Alexandria, VA: TESOL.

Johns, A. M. 1991. English for specific purposes (ESP): Its history and contributions. In M. Celce-Murcia, ed., *Teaching English as a Second or Foreign Language.* Boston: Heinle and Heinle.

Johns, A. M. 1993. Written argumentation for real audiences: Suggestions for teacher research and classroom practice. *TESOL Quarterly* 27 (1): 75–90.

Johns, A. M. 1994. Issues in ESP for the 90s. In R. Khoo, ed., *LSP—Problems and Prospects.* Anthology Series, no. 13. Singapore: SEAMEO Regional Language Centre.

Johns, A. M. 1995a. Genre and pedagogical purposes. *Journal of Second Language Writing* 4 (2): 181–90.

Johns, A. M. 1995b. Teaching classroom and authentic genres: Initiating students into academic cultures and discourses. In D. Belcher and G. Braine, eds., *Academic Writing in a Second Language: Essays on Research and Pedagogy.* Norwood, NJ: Ablex.

Johns, A. M. 1997. *Text, Role, and Context: Developing Academic Literacies.* Cambridge: Cambridge University Press.

Johns, A. M. 1998. The visual and the verbal: A case study in macroeconomics. *English for Specific Purposes* 17 (2): 183–97.

Jordan, R. R. 1997. *English for Academic Purposes: A Guide and Resource Book for Teachers.* Cambridge: Cambridge University Press.

Joyce, H. 1992. *Workplace Texts in the Language Classroom*. Sydney: New South Wales Adult Migrant Education Service.

Kanpol, B. 1990. Political applied linguistics and postmodernism: Towards an engagement of similarity with difference. *Issues in Applied Linguistics* 1 (2): 238–50.

Kay, H. 1995. Whither genre? Paper presented at the BAAL/CUP workshop/seminar on genre, Sheffield University, July.

Kay, H., and T. Dudley-Evans. 1998. Genre: What teachers think. *ELT Journal* 52 (4): 308–14.

Kennedy, G. 1992. Preferred ways of putting things with implications for language teaching. In J. Svartvik, ed., *Directions in Corpus Linguistics*. Berlin: Mouton de Gruyter.

King, S., and B. Paltridge 1991. *Context: An Australian Intensive English Course*. Melbourne: Longman Australia.

Klippel, F. 1984. *Keep Talking*. Cambridge: Cambridge University Press.

Knapp, P., and M. Watkins. 1994. *Context—Text—Grammar: Teaching the Genres and Grammar of School Writing in Infants and Primary Classrooms*. Sydney: Text Productions.

Kowal, M., and M. Swain. 1994. Using collaborative language production tasks to promote students' language awareness. *Language Awareness* 3:73–93.

Kress, G., and T. van Leeuwen. 1990. *Reading Images*. Geelong, Australia: Deakin University Press.

Kress, G., and T. van Leeuwen. 1996. *Reading Images: The Grammar of Visual Design*. London: Routledge.

Kubota, R. 2000. Politics of cultural difference in second language writing. Keynote presentation at the Symposium on Second Language Writing, Purdue University, Lafayette, IN, September.

Kusel, P. A. 1992. Rhetorical approaches to the study and composition of academic essays. *System* 20 (4): 457–69.

Labov, W., and J. Waletzky. 1967. Narrative analysis: Oral versions of personal experiences. In J. Helm, ed., *Essays on the Verbal and Visual Arts*. Washington, DC: University of Washington Press.

Levine, D., and M. B. Adelman. 1982. *Beyond Language: Intercultural Communication for English as a Second Language*. Englewood Cliffs, NJ: Prentice-Hall.

Levine, D., J. Baxter, and P. McNulty. 1987. *The Culture Puzzle: Cross-Cultural Communication for English as a Second Language.* Englewood Cliffs, NJ: Prentice-Hall.

Littlewood, W. 1981. *Communicative Language Teaching.* Cambridge: Cambridge University Press.

Ljung, M. 1991. Swedish TEFL meets reality. In S. Johansson and A.-B. Stenstrom, eds., *English Computer Corpora.* Berlin: Mouton de Gruyter.

Lowe, I. 1996. Non-verbal devices in pre-university science: The extent of correspondence between English and French. *English for Specific Purposes* 15 (3): 217–32.

Luke, A. 1996. Genres of power? Literacy education and the production of capital. In R. Hasan and G. Williams, eds., *Literacy in Society.* London: Longman.

Mackay, S. 1995. Using a genre approach in the EFL reading classroom. *EA Journal* 13 (1): 7–13.

Macken, M., and D. Slade. 1993. Assessment: A foundation for effective learning in the school context. In B. Cope and M. Kalantzis, eds., *The Powers of Literacy: A Genre Approach to Teaching Writing.* London: Falmer.

Maier, P. 1992. Politeness strategies in business letters by native and non-native English speakers. *English for Specific Purposes* 11 (3): 189–205.

Mamouney, R. 1989. A positive framework for assessing written language in the teaching/learning cycle. In *Working with Genre: Papers from the 1989 LERN Conference, University of Technology, Sydney.* Leichhart, New South Wales: Common Ground.

Martin, J. R. 1984. Language, register, and genre. In F. Christie, ed., *Language Studies: Children's Writing, Reader.* Geelong, Australia: Deakin University Press.

Martin, J. R. 1989. *Factual Writing: Exploring and Challenging Social Reality.* Oxford: Oxford University Press.

Martin, J. R. 1992. *English Text: System and Structure.* Amsterdam and Philadelphia: John Benjamins.

Martin, J. R. 1993. Genre and literacy—modeling context in educational linguistics. *Annual Review of Applied Linguistics* 13:141–72.

Martin, J. R., and J. Rothery. 1986. What a functional approach to the writing task can show about "good writing." In B. Couture, ed., *Functional Approaches to Writing.* Norwood, NJ: Ablex.

Master, P. 1987. Generic *the* in *Scientific American. English for Specific Purposes* 6 (2): 165–86.

Mauranen, A. 1993. Contrastive ESP rhetoric: Metatext in Finnish-English economics text. *English for Specific Purposes* 12 (1): 3–22.

McCarthy, M. 1991. *Discourse Analysis for Language Teachers.* Cambridge: Cambridge University Press.

McCarthy, M., and R. Carter. 1994. *Language as Discourse: Perspectives for Language Teaching.* London: Longman.

Miller, C. R. 1984. Genre as social action. *Quarterly Journal of Speech* 70:151–67. Reprinted in A. Freedman and P. Medway, eds., *Genre and the New Rhetoric* (London: Taylor and Francis, 1994).

Miller, C. R. 1994. Rhetorical community: The cultural basis of genre. In A. Freedman and P. Medway, eds., *Genre and the New Rhetoric.* London: Taylor and Francis.

Miller, T. 1998. Visual persuasion: A comparison of visuals in academic texts and the popular press. *English for Specific Purposes* 17 (1): 29–46.

Mustafa, Z. 1995. The effect of genre awareness on linguistic transfer. *English for Specific Purposes* 14 (3): 247–56.

Myers, G. 2000. Powerpoints: Technology, lectures, and changing genres. In A. Trosberg, ed., *Analyzing Professional Genres.* Amsterdam and Philadelphia: John Benjamins.

Nolasco, R., and L. Arthur. 1987. *Conversation.* Oxford: Oxford University Press.

Nunan, D. 1991. *Language Teaching Methodology: A Textbook for Teachers.* New York: Prentice-Hall.

Nunan, D. 1999. *Second Language Teaching and Learning.* Boston: Heinle and Heinle.

Nunan, D., and J. Burton. 1989. *National Curriculum Project: English in the Workplace.* Sydney: NCECTR, Macquarie University.

Ohta, A. M. 2000. Rethinking interaction in SLA: Developmentally appropriate assistance in the zone of proximal development and the acquisition of L2 grammar. In J. P. Lantolf, ed., *Sociocultural Theory and Second Language Learning.* Oxford: Oxford University Press.

Olsher, D. 1998. How's your genre awareness? In P. Master and D. Brinton, eds., *New Ways in English for Specific Purposes.* Alexandria, VA: TESOL.

Orr, T. 1998. Creating lifetime genre files. In P. Master and D. Brinton, eds., *New Ways in English for Specific Purposes.* Alexandria, VA: TESOL.

Paltridge, B. 1987. Keeping a Conversation Going. *Prospect* 3 (1): 103–8.

Paltridge, B. 1992. EAP placement testing: An integrated approach. *English for Specific Purposes* 11 (3): 243–68.

Paltridge, B. 1995a. Analysing genre: A relational perspective. *System* 23 (4): 503–11.

Paltridge, B. 1995b. Genre and the notion of prototype. *Prospect* 10 (3): 28–34.

Paltridge, B. 1995c. An integrated approach to language program development. *English Teaching Forum* 33 (3): 41–44.

Paltridge, B. 1996. Genre, text type, and the language learning classroom. *ELT Journal* 50 (3): 237–43.

Paltridge, B. 1998. Observation, feedback, and setting individual learning goals. In J. D. Brown, ed., *New Ways of Classroom Assessment*. Alexandria, VA: TESOL.

Paltridge, B. 1999. Reading across the curriculum: A genre-based perspective. In D. Short, ed., *New Ways in Teaching English at the Secondary Level*. Alexandria, VA: TESOL.

Paltridge, B. 2002. Genre, text type, and the EAP classroom. In A. Johns, ed., *Genre in the Classroom: Multiple Perspectives*. Mahwah, NJ: Lawrence Erlbaum.

Pennycook, A. 1996. TESOL and critical literacies: Modern, post, or neo? *TESOL Quarterly* 30 (1): 163–71.

Pennycook, A. 1997. Critical applied linguistics and education. In R. Wodak and D. Corson, eds., *Encyclopedia of Language and Education,* vol. 1. Dordrecht: Kluwer.

Plum, G. 1988. Text and contextual conditioning in spoken English: A genre-based approach. Ph.D. diss., University of Sydney.

Prior, P. 1995. Redefining the task: An ethnographic examination of writing and response in graduate seminars. In D. Belcher and G. Braine, eds., *Academic Writing in a Second Language: Essays on Research and Pedagogy.* Norwood, NJ: Ablex.

Prior, P. 1998. *Writing/Disciplinarity: A Sociohistoric Account of Literate Activity in the Academy.* Mahwah, NJ: Lawrence Erlbaum.

Raimes, A. 1991. Out of the woods: Emerging traditions in the teaching of writing. *TESOL Quarterly* 25 (3): 407–30.

Raimes, A. 1998. Teaching writing. *Annual Review of Applied Linguistics* 18:142–67.

Ramani, E., T. Chacko, S. J. Singh, and E. H. Glendinning. 1988. An ethnographic approach to syllabus design: A case study of the Indian Institute of Science, Bangalore. *English for Specific Purposes* 7 (1): 81–90.

Ranney, S. 1992. Learning a new script: An exploration of sociolinguistic competence. *Applied Linguistics* 13 (1): 25–50.

Raymond, P. 1999. Student beliefs about written genres. Paper presented at the Second Language Research Forum, University of Minnesota, September.

Reppen, R. 1995. A genre-based approach to content writing instruction. *TESOL Journal* 4 (2): 32–35.

Richards, J. C., J. Platt, and H. Platt. 1992. *Longman Dictionary of Language Teaching and Applied Linguistics.* New ed. Essex: Longman.

Richards, J. C., and T. Rodgers. 1986. *Approaches and Methods in Language Teaching: A Description and Analysis.* Cambridge: Cambridge University Press.

Richards, J. C., and R. Schmidt. 1983. Conversational analysis. In J. C. Richards and R. Schmidt, eds., *Language and Communication.* London: Longman.

Riggenbach, H. 1999. *Discourse Analysis in the Language Classroom.* Vol. 1, *The Spoken Language.* Ann Arbor: University of Michigan Press.

Robinson, P. 1991. *ESP Today: A Practitioner's Guide.* London: Prentice-Hall.

Rosch, E. 1983. Prototype classification and logical classification: The two systems. In E. K. Scholnick, ed., *New Trends in Conceptual Representation: Challenges to Piaget's Theory?* Hillsdale, NJ: Lawrence Erlbaum.

Rothery, J. 1986. Teaching writing in the primary school: A genre-based approach to the development of writing abilities. Working Papers in Linguistics, no. 4, University of Sydney.

Rothery, J. 1990. Story writing in primary school: Assessing narrative-type genres. Ph.D. diss., University of Sydney.

Sartain, S. 1995. Letter to the editor. *Sunday Age,* 30 April, 16.

Sengupta. S. 1999. Rhetorical consciousness-raising in the L2 reading classroom. *Journal of Second Language Writing* 8 (3): 291–319.

Shih, M. 1999. More than practicing language: Communicative reading and writing for Asian settings. *TESOL Journal* 8 (4): 20–25.

Silva, T., M. Reichelt, and J. Lax-Farr. 1994. Writing instruction for ESL graduate students: Examining issues and raising questions. *ELT Journal* 48 (3): 197–204.

Simpson, R., and J. M. Swales, eds. 2001. *Corpus Linguistics in North America.* Ann Arbor: University of Michigan Press.

Smart, G. 1992. Exploring the social dimension of a workplace genre and the implications for teaching. *Carleton Papers in Applied Language Studies* 9:35–46.

Spack, R. 1998. Initiating ESL students into the academic discourse community: How far should we go? In V. Zamel and R. Spack, eds., *Negotiating Academic Literacies.* Mahwah, NJ: Lawrence Erlbaum.

Swales, J. M. 1981. Aspects of article introductions. Birmingham, UK: University of Aston Language Studies Unit.

Swales, J. M. 1986. A genre-based approach to language across the curriculum. In M. L. Tickoo, ed., *Language across the Curriculum.* Anthology Series, no. 15. Singapore: SEAMEO Regional Language Centre.

Swales, J. M. 1990. *Genre Analysis. English in Academic and Research Settings.* Cambridge: Cambridge University Press.

Swales, J. M. 1993. Genre and engagement. *Revue Belge de Philologie et d'Histoire* 71 (3): 689–98.

Swales, J. M. 1995. The role of the textbook in EAP writing research. *English for Specific Purposes* 14 (1): 3–18.

Swales, J. M. 1996. Occluded genres in the academy: The case of the submission letter. In E. Ventola and A. Mauranen, eds., *Academic Writing: Intercultural and Textual Issues.* Amsterdam and Philadelphia: John Benjamins.

Swales, J. M. 1998. *Other Floors, Other Voices: A Textography of a Small University Building.* Mahwah, NJ: Lawrence Erlbaum.

Swales, J. M. 2000a. Languages for specific purposes. *Annual Review of Applied Linguistics* 20:59–76.

Swales, J. M. 2000b. Further reflections on genre and ESL academic writing. Abstract of the keynote presentation to the Symposium on Second Language Writing, Purdue University, Lafayette, IN, September.

Swales, J. M., and C. B. Feak. 1994. *Academic Writing for Graduate Students: Essential Tasks and Skills.* Ann Arbor: University of Michigan Press.

Swales, J. M., and C. B. Feak. 2000. *English in Today's Research World: A Writing Guide.* Ann Arbor: University of Michigan Press.

Swales, J. M., and S. Hyon. 1994. Genres of power. In A. C. Purves, ed., *Encyclopedia of English Studies and Language Arts: A Project of the National Council of Teachers of English.* New York: Scholastic.

Tarone, E. S. Dwyer, S. Gillette, and V. Icke. 1981. On the use of the passive in two astrophysics journal papers. *ESP Journal* 1 (2): 123–40. Reprinted in J. Swales, ed., *Episodes in ESP* (Oxford: Pergamon, 1985).

Taylor, G., and T. Chen. 1991. Linguistic, cultural, and subcultural issues in contrastive discourse analysis: Anglo-American and Chinese scientific texts. *Applied Linguistics* 12 (3): 319–36.

Tedick, D. J. 1990. ESL writing assessment: Subject-matter knowledge and its impact on performance. *English for Specific Purposes* 9:123–43.

Tharp, R. G., and R. Gallimore 1991. *The Instructional Conversation: Teaching and Learning in Social Activity.* New York: Cambridge University Press.

Thomas, J. 1983. Cross-cultural pragmatic failure. *Applied Linguistics* 4 (2): 91–112.

Thompson, S. 1994. Frameworks and contexts: A genre-based approach to analysing lecture introductions. *English for Specific Purposes* 13 (2): 171–86.

Thornbury, S. 1997. *About Language: Tasks for Teachers of English.* Cambridge: Cambridge University Press.

Thornbury, S. 2000. *How to Teach Grammar.* London: Longman.

Threadgold, T. 1989. Talking about genre: Ideologies and incompatible discourses. *Cultural Studies* 3:101–27.

Tickoo, M. L. 1994. Approaches to ESP: Arguing a paradigm shift. In R. Khoo, ed., *LSP—Problems and Prospects.* Anthology Series, no. 13. Singapore: SEAMEO Regional Language Centre.

Tribble, C. 1996. *Writing.* Oxford: Oxford University Press.

Ur, P. 1988. *Grammar Practice Activities.* Cambridge: Cambridge University Press.

Ur, P. 1996. *A Course in Language Teaching: Practice and Theory.* Cambridge: Cambridge University Press.

Vygotsky, L. S. 1978. *Mind in Society.* Cambridge: Harvard University Press.

Wallace, C. 1992. *Reading.* Oxford: Oxford University Press.

Weissberg, R. 1993. The graduate seminar: Another research-process genre. *English for Specific Purposes* 12 (1): 23–35.

Weissberg, R., and S. Buker. 1990. *Writing Up Research: Experimental Report Writing for Students of English.* Englewood Cliffs, NJ: Prentice-Hall Regents.

Widdowson, H. G. 1983. *Learning Purpose and Language Use.* Oxford: Oxford University Press.

Wittgenstein, L. 1953. *Philosophical Investigations.* Oxford: Oxford University Press.

Wood, D., J. S. Bruner, and G. Ross. 1976. The role of tutoring in problem-solving. *Journal of Child Psychology and Psychiatry* 17:89–100.

Zamel, V. 1998. Questioning academic discourse. In V. Zamel and R. Spack, eds., *Negotiating Academic Literacies.* Mahwah, NJ: Lawrence Erlbaum.

Subject Index

Author Index